GROWING
SPIRITUAL
REDWOODS

Growing Spiritual Redwoods

William M. Easum and Thomas G. Bandy

Abingdon Press
Nashville

GROWING SPIRITUAL REDWOODS

Library of Congress Cataloging-in-Publication Data

Easum, William M., 1939–
   Growing spiritual redwoods / William M. Easum and Thomas Bandy.
   p. cm.
   Includes index.
   ISBN 0-687-33600-7 (alk. paper)
   1. Pastoral theology. 2. Spiritual life—Christianity. 3. United States
   —Church history—20th century. I. Bandy, Thomas G., 1950–
   II. Title.
   BV4011.E329   1997
   250—dc21   97-37034
                                                                          CIP

98 99 00 01 02 03 04 05 06 — 10 9 8 7 6 5 4 3

MANUFACTURED IN THE UNITED STATES OF AMERICA

VISTAS

Appreciation

T his book is the result of labors of love on the part of many people. We have sought to synthesize and articulate their learnings for the benefit of growing churches everywhere.

We are indebted to the many Spiritual Redwood congregations
emerging all around us in Canada and the United States, most
notably Prince of Peace Lutheran Church in Burnsville, Minneso-
ta, and Christ United Methodist Church in Ft. Lauderdale, Florida. Our association with these churches has taught us much about
the new species of Christian organism emerging on the brink of a
new era. We are also indebted to groups of midwives, nurses, and
health-care professionals throughout North America. We give our
thanks to our publisher for having the courage to use this book in
their new electronic market.

Of course, we give our thanks to our spouses and families for
their unending patience and generosity as we have given time to
the research and work of this project. Without the prayers and
encouragement of our loved ones and friends we could do nothing.

Finally, we celebrate the courageous examples of thousands of
lay servants of Jesus Christ throughout the world for the inspiration they have given us. We thank God for allowing us to be part
of the spiritual flow that is moving through the world. We pray

that there will be time and vision for innumerable established churches to become a part of that flow.

Bill Easum
Tom Bandy

Bill Easum and Tom Bandy are available for speaking engagements and local church consultations. You may reach them at:

Bill Easum
E-mail: easum@easum.com
Voice mail: 512-749-5364
Fax: 512-749-5800

Tom Bandy
Phone and fax: 519-823-2596
E-mail: TGBandy@aol.com

VISTAS

Sightings from the Top of the Tree

VISTA ONE

Welcome!

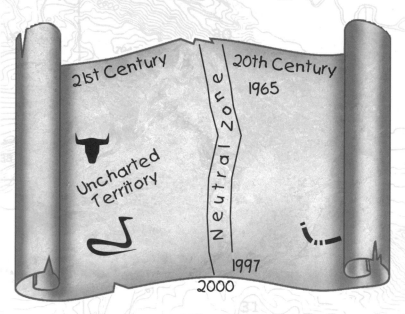

You are standing at the edge of the future. All the territory in front of you is an uncharted forest. The forest is extremely dense and filled with obstacles. See if you are brave enough to find a path to the twenty-first century.

W e share a vision. It is a vision that has emerged for each of us from different churches, in different denominations, in different places, and yet from remarkably parallel experiences. It is a vision that has survived personal struggles as pastors and consultants with declining congregations and dinosaur bureaucracies, and that has borne fruit with thriving congregations and bold new leadership. It is a vision that has been refined and affirmed in personal pastoral experience, and in literally thousands of consultations across North America. It is a vision that has been controversial to some, and invigorating to many, because it has led us into "dancing with dinosaurs," "kicking corporate habits," and "eating gourmet burgers made from sacred cows." It is a vision *to live and let thrive!*

Together we have asked countless congregations and church members a single question: *"How would you describe your spiritual journey?"* Members of declining churches say something like this:

I grew up in church because it was what my parents wanted. I attended Sunday school, but dropped out after I was confirmed. I attended youth group, but dropped out after high school. When I got married, had kids, and relocated, we looked for the branch of our denomination and rejoined. I was soon asked to join a committee, and my wife was asked to teach Sunday school. Later I was invited to serve with the Finance Committee and the Trustees, while my wife graduated to the Personnel Committee. I became Chairman of the Committee, then Chairman of the governing body. My wife became President of the women's group. We held those positions until retiring from church work. We've done our part, our children are grown, and now it's up to them. They are the future of the church . . . but somehow they don't seem as committed as we were.

Participants in thriving churches say something like this:

My parents weren't very religious, so I only went to church Christmas and Easter. Those services were some of the most boring times I can remember. After my parents got divorced, we stopped going unless Grandma was visiting. I got married, had a kid, got the kid baptized in Grandma's church, and then got divorced. The divorce was devastating. It must have shown, because a friend suggested that I attend a group that met during the week in her home. It was sponsored by her church. Was I shocked! I met real people talking about real issues in my life. In a few months, I began attending worship at her church. It was nothing like I remembered. People were actually enjoy-

ing themselves. In time, Christ became a part of my life. I married someone in the church, and we began serving one of the outreach missions. Three years later we officially joined the church. Our relationships with others and with God have steadily grown. It's been a great experience, and we expect it to get even better.

These contrasting statements epitomize the profound difference between a declining and a thriving church. What is revealed in them is not the difference between programs, strategic plans, or denominational polities, but the contrast of two distinctly different understandings of what it means to "be the church."

"What exactly have Christians been 'called out' to be and do?"

Most Christian leaders know that the Greek word "ecclesia," which we translate "church," means literally *"a calling out."* Christians have been "called out" from the world as a distinct people. The recognition of this distinctive identity is shared by both declining and thriving churches. The question that confronts Christians on the brink of the twenty-first century is this: *"What exactly have Christians been 'called out' to be and do?"* The answer to this question makes all the difference.

Christians in dying churches believe that they have been "called out" to form a distinct society. They see themselves as an institution in which the members all follow certain rules, undertake various institutional responsibilities, and all enjoy specific privileges. The church is a club to which they can retreat for personal refreshment, and in which their needs can be met by a personal chaplain. Therefore, they worry about raising money to pay the chaplain's salary and to maintain the property as a safe haven from the world. When they think about new members, they often do so with a view to having help in paying the bills. They seek to build great endowments, or at least substantial emergency funds, so that they can survive the loss of long-standing members. They compete with other "clubs" by offering superior privileges for membership and more attention from salaried servants, or offering lower membership dues. Their attitude is always *"Let's take care of our members first, then, with any resources left over, we'll go after the lost."* Their strategy is always *"First bring the lost into our institution; then, once they are members, they can enjoy the benefits of the club.*" On the brink of the twenty-first century, they are increasingly filled with worry about the survival of their church and confused over why fewer and fewer people want to join the church.

Christians in growing churches believe that they have been "called out" to form a distinct witness. Bill spoke about this witness in *The Church Growth Handbook*. Tom spoke of this witness in *Kicking Habits*. This witness is about Jesus, not their church or their denomination. They see themselves as a community in which the participants all experience a constant connection with Jesus, enjoy "fruits of the Spirit" which come from relationship with Jesus, and purposely reach out as "the Body of Christ." With this company of companions, they continually deepen their faith and hope, grow in awareness of self and mission, and share love with complete strangers. Their attitude is always *"Let's bring abundant life to others first, and then we, too, will have abundant life."* Their strategy is always *"First go out among the publics of modern culture to forge new links with Jesus, and then invite people into companionship with the Body of Christ."* On the brink of the twenty-first century, they worry about finding the best vehicles to communicate the gospel to a diverse world, and wonder at the multitudes who are eager to listen.

The choice today is similar to the choice of the faithful in the first century.

On the one hand, Christians can become a *righteous remnant*. They can follow the Essenes to form a distinct society, retreating into fortresses and caves of institutional elitism, self-righteously preserving what they understand to be "good" worship, "pure" doctrine, or "correct" ideology. They can initiate decreasing numbers of like-minded believers into the secrets of the society, and store their wealth in clay jars and certified bank deposits. They can shut themselves within a spiritual "Masada," besieged by culture round about, and eventually choose to die rather than "surrender."

On the other hand, Christians can become an *apostolic witness*. They can follow Paul, Silas, Lydia, and Priscilla into a mission to the Gentiles, advancing into public places and personal conversations, joyously sharing a relationship with Jesus that bears the fruits of abundant life. They can bring increasing numbers of spiritual seekers into a companionship that deepens faith, builds awareness of destiny, and equips mission. They can surrender their certificates of deposit and ecclesiastical fortresses, and transform the surrounding culture one conversation at a time, one day at a time.

The contrasts between declining and thriving churches existing side-by-side in North America on the brink of the twenty-first century are often readily apparent. To declining-church members, these contrasts may be mystifying, threatening, and painful. To thriving-church participants, these same contrasts may be obvious, empowering, and exciting.

Members of Declining Congregations Are:	Participants in Thriving Congregations Are:
Committed to the church	Committed to Christ
Managing committees	Deploying missions
Holding offices	Doing hands-on ministries
Making decisions	Making disciples
Trained for membership	On a lifelong quest for quality
Serving at the church	Serving in the world
Preoccupied with raising money	Preoccupied with rescuing people
Doing church work	Finding personal fulfillment
Retiring from church work	Pursuing constant personal growth
Surveying internal needs	Sensitizing themselves to community needs
Eager to know everyone	Eager for everyone to know God
Loyal to one another	Drawn to the unchurched
Building faith on information	Building faith on experience with Christ
Perpetuating a heritage	Visioning a future

Perhaps the most dramatic contrast has been revealed whenever we have shared these lists with congregational groups across North America. Declining churches want to do everything on the right-hand side, *without letting go* of anything on the left-hand side. Thriving churches want wholeheartedly to do everything on the right-hand side and *are prepared to let go* of everything on the left-hand side.

The Body of Christ will sacrifice anything and everything—property, offices, financial security, traditional music, familiar heritage—for the sake of Jesus and the gospel.

> The Body of Christ will sacrifice anything and everything—property, offices, financial security, traditional music, familiar heritage—for the sake of Jesus and the gospel.

Living on the Edge of Tomorrow

Not only have we asked congregations and church members key questions, but we have asked pastors and church leaders key questions. Once again, the contrasts between declining-church leaders and thriving-church leaders have been dramatic. Here are some examples:

"Why did you start a day-care center?"

Declining-church leaders said: *"Because it provides a good service to the community, and brings in some rental income for facilities unused through the week."* Thriving-church leaders said: *"Because it is an important way into the homes and hearts of unchurched people to share the transforming power of Jesus Christ."*

"Why does your church have a stewardship campaign?"

Declining-church leaders said: *"We need money to address the operational deficit, create more programs, and save money for the future."* Thriving-church leaders said: *"We want to help people grow spiritually, and equip people to share the gospel around the world."*

"Why did you write a new mission statement?"

Declining-church leaders said: *"We need to celebrate our heritage, organize all the committees into a better system of management, and hold people accountable for their actions."* Thriving-church leaders said: *"We need to express our core vision with words, motivate our people for immediate ministry, and lay the foundation of trust for any eruption of the Spirit people want to try."*

One thriving-church leader said it in a nutshell. Bill asked her: *"How do you decide what ministries to begin?"* She answered: *"We tell people that if the Lord lays it on your heart today, you can do it tonight, and tell us about it tomorrow!"*

Living on the edge of tomorrow requires more daring than ever before. We are living on the edge of a millennium, of an era, of an age. Tomorrow will not simply be an extension of yesterday. It will be more discontinuous with yesterday. In *Kicking Habits*, Tom described the hidden addictions that must be addressed if we are ever to leap across the chasm. You can assess the readiness of your own congregation to reach people in the twenty-first century by asking questions such as these:

1. Are you committed to Jesus Christ . . . or to a particular doctrine, denomination, or church?

We have found that thriving churches have let go the idols of dogma, polity, and property. Nothing is important except the gospel.

2. Do you speak of faith as an experience with Christ . . . or as a heritage that you protect?

We have found that thriving churches speak of personal transformations, and growing, healthy relationships. They enjoy sharing faith in public.

3. Do you believe that ministry is to make disciples and missionaries . . . not decisions and members?

We have found that thriving churches have let go the energy pits of institutional management and recruitment. Ministry creates lay ministries.

4. Do you design mission for the needs and yearnings of the public . . . or the needs of church members?

We have found that thriving churches shun codependent relationships. They help others by equipping them to look beyond themselves and to give life away in the name of Jesus Christ.

5. Do you quickly grasp unexpected opportunities . . . or do you worry about rules and procedures?

We have found that thriving churches minimize control. They even break rules and bend procedures, if that is what it takes to do the right thing now.

6. Do you promote mentoring or midwifing relationships . . . or do you just nominate people to offices?

We have found that thriving churches minimize administration. They focus energy on coaching others to self-discovery, and equipping excellent ministry.

7. Do you build small groups . . . or wrestle with power cliques?

We have found that thriving churches avoid cliques that control leadership, fight change, or socialize selectively. They build spiritual, mutual-support groups.

8. Do you worship with excited expectancy . . . or do you worship in order to discharge a duty?

We have found that thriving churches never watch the clock in worship, nor do they try to cram all of their faith expression into one hour of worship. Anything can happen in the lives of the worshiping participants.

9. Do you expect newcomers to be accompanied by spiritual guides . . . or do you just wait for them at the door?

We have found that thriving churches never just advertise and wait. They invite and guide friends, neighbors, associates, relatives, and perfect strangers to church.

10. Do you value changing lives . . . or do you value belonging to an institution?

We have found that thriving churches talk discipleship, not membership. They have a passion for transforming life, by transforming lives.

11. Do you ask for radical commitment . . . or do you not expect much from people?

We have found that thriving churches take John 14:12 seriously and expect people to strive to live as Jesus lived.

If you affirmed the first part of most questions, your congregation is poised to grow in the twenty-first century. If you affirmed some of the first parts, and some of the second parts, you have just targeted your agenda for change. If you affirmed mostly the second parts of the questions, convert the entire church budget into one vast "Memorial Fund" to pay for the coming funeral . . . *or* redirect all your congregational energies to seeking God's vision for your future.

In every field of ambitious endeavor today, leaders must answer the question, *"What business are we really in?"* Success will depend on their ability to answer that question. The Christian answer will always depend on an even more basic question: *"To whom do we really belong?"* Christians belong both to Jesus and to the community. Our business is Jesus and community. To grow more like Jesus; to share what Jesus has done in our lives with others; to develop a community of love, hope, and trust in the midst of the yearnings of culture. That is our business. The purpose of any church is not merely to remember the story, but to be and share the story.

Growing Spiritual Redwoods

We like to use organic, relational metaphors to describe thriving churches. In *Sacred Cows Make Gourmet Burgers*, Bill spoke of the quantum, relational church of the future. In *Kicking Habits: Welcome Relief for Addicted Churches*, Tom spoke of church growth in the pediatric metaphors of the thriving church. In this book, we present a new metaphor. It is organic, dynamic, relational, natural . . . and Big! It is the *Spiritual Redwood.*

Christians all across North America are asking one another if there is hope for the church. We believe that there is abundant hope for the Body of Christ. There is great hope for individual churches with the courage to be reorganized, redirected, and systemically transformed. There is far less hope for denominations, and no hope at all for religious bureaucracies. The immediate future will reveal centers of spiritual strength in the midst of closing and amalgamating church institutions. These centers will tower above the decaying religious bureaucracies, to become inspirational models and teaching centers.

These manifestations of the Body of Christ rise up like Spiritual Redwoods amid the forest of change. One can sense their greatness, strength, magnetism, and destiny. They stand tall, reach far, embrace much . . . and cast long shadows.

This book is devoted to the description of the Spiritual Redwood. The research and consultations that we have done across North America convince us that churches that grow to become spiritual giants in the twenty-first century will:

- base everything on their experience of the transforming power of Jesus;
- organize themselves around strong team leaders and fulfilling lay ministries;
- devote themselves to experiencing God through indigenous worship;
- be led by visionary leaders who create an environment of change;
- focus themselves on making disciples;
- devote themselves to reaching out to the community with valuable help.

These spiritual giants will no longer set the mission agenda "from above," recruiting people to committees to do what the institution wants them to do. They will set the mission agenda "from below," releasing gifted and called people to do crazy, creative, caring, and spirit-filled things with excellence.

> Creating the environment that will grow Spiritual Redwoods is the primary task of leadership in our time.

We write this book in the belief that Spiritual Redwoods are not born or built . . . *they are grown.* Creating the environment that will grow such organisms is the primary task of leadership in our time.

VISTA TWO

Standing Tall in the Forest

The Old Saying

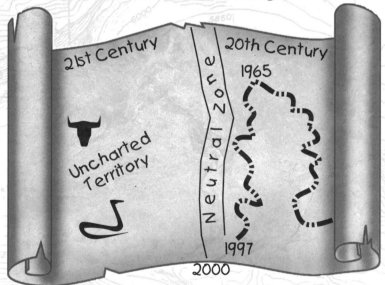

Finding the
right paths through the
forest requires a better view
of the horizon.

T here is an old saying that has often been used by strategic planners to describe churches unable to plan for the future: *"They can't see the forest for all the trees!"* Christian congregations become so preoccupied with the details of management, maintenance, and survival, that they lose sight of the "big picture." Their original purpose for existing, and their broader connections with the community, become lost. Busy coping with year-end operational deficits, they fail to identify emerging mission needs. Absorbed by individual membership demands and personality conflicts, they fail to be relevant to the public. Enchanted by the latest theological trends, fixated on single ideological or dogmatic issues, and entrapped by addictions to pipe organs and property, these churches cannot even imagine a thriving future. *They can't see the forest for all the trees.*

The problem with this old saying is that it is no longer adequate to explain the depth and breadth of the challenge facing churches in the twenty-first century. Nor is it adequate any longer to guide churches to engage in healthy long-range planning! This old saying is *merely three-dimensional.* It assumes that a careful survey of the full height, length, and width of the forest, in place of looking at just the trees, will be adequate to plan for the future. It assumes that church development is a matter of measuring geographic, demographic, psychographic, and financial trends. It assumes:

- that the forest will "hold still" long enough to be studied;
- that the forest will "stay still" long enough for the church to adjust itself to it;
- that the forest will "be still" and essentially unchanging.

None of these assumptions is valid for the twenty-first century. This is why "strategic planning," as it has been known in the twentieth century, is dead.

Futuring the church now must consider *the fourth dimension of TIME.* The forest will no longer "hold still" long enough to be thoroughly researched. Blink once, and you have to start over. Every moment is a revolution. By the time the church locates a new clearing in which to plant itself, the forest has moved on.

Futuring the church must now consider *the fifth dimension of CYBERSPACE.* The forest will no longer "stay still" long enough for the church to simply adjust to it. Information is moving so quickly, and so comprehensively, that personal and social realities are evolving at exponential speeds. The definitions of identity now include process itself.

1500–1960	"I think, therefore I am."
1960–1990	"I feel, therefore I am."
1990–?	"I compute and simulate, therefore I am."

Nuance and evolution are so important to identity in the twenty-first century, that the simplest creature of the forest can only be described as "Version 1.1."

Finally, futuring the church must now consider *the sixth dimension of GRACE*. Those tornadoes, floods, and fires we jokingly describe as "acts of God," *really are acts of GOD!* The forest will no longer "be still" and be essentially the same. God's power breaks into the forest to shatter old forms in entirely unexpected ways. Programmatic change is no longer the divine plan. Systemic change is the divine plan. The church that just tinkers with more creative stewardship, or merely tries to "reach the youth," in order to re-create what worked in the past, not only finds itself left behind by the forest . . . it finds itself left behind by God.

The New Maxim

This book replaces the old saying, "You can't see the forest for all the trees!" with a new one applicable to the twenty-first century:

"You can't see the future of forestry,
unless you climb the tallest tree!"

We believe that, to grow strong and healthy churches, it is no longer sufficient to see the forest. You have to understand the changing nature of *forestry*. You have to understand how the forest is rapidly changing . . . and how the transforming power of God is creating whole new species of trees . . . and how church leadership that nurtures dynamic growth is a whole new kind of forestry! It is no longer just the trees or forest that count, but the relationships between the trees.

The "forest" is a metaphor for culture, the public, or people and the environments and yearnings in which they live. This "forest" is incredibly diverse, and growing more diverse every minute. All the rules of the "forest" are changing . . . and they are completely different from the supposed "civilization" of the twentieth-century institutional church.

We also believe that, to grow strong and healthy churches, you must climb the tallest trees. You must seek out the "Spiritual Redwoods." You must find those trees in the forest that are growing and thriving, brimming with wholeness and health, extending branches and leaves ever outward, sheltering an enormous diversity of God's creatures within their spiritual environment.

To find the right paths through the forest to the twenty-first century requires a panoramic view of the future.

The "Spiritual Redwood" is a metaphor for the new species of dynamic Christian organism, led by visionary spiritual leaders, that is learning to flourish in the changed environment of the twenty-first century. From its heights you can see the changing trends of the forest, and from its roots you can feel the changing nuances of each creature of the forest.

This book is all about the emerging church transformation maxim of the twenty-first century: "You can't see the future of forestry, unless you climb the tallest tree."

Finding the Right Paths Through a Pre-Christian World

The church has always been wary of the forest. Its deep shadows and sudden illuminations seemed to encourage all manner of talk about gods, goddesses, and demons. Fertility cults, competing spiritualities, mystical experiences, and supernatural speculations surround authentic Christian faith. In the past, the church tended to attack the forest, chopping it down to make way for cathedrals of dogmatic or ideological correctness. Church leaders erected multiple gateways to guard the entrances to their denominationally

homogeneous churches. Hurdles of baptism counseling, membership training, and institutional assimilation ensured that none of the
mud of the forest ever made it into the "City of God." Yet as the
structures and institutions of the twentieth century crumble, the
forest infringes upon society once again.

Just finding your way through the forest, in order to discover the
Spiritual Redwoods, can be a challenging prospect. Yet church
leaders and spiritual seekers are setting out as never before to
explore new territory, and grow a twenty-first-century version of
the "Body of Christ." Before you even start, you need to equip
yourself with a different map.

Many have described this new era as the "postindustrial society,"
"the postsecular age," or the "postmodern world." The trouble is
the maps they draw of the twenty-first century are always "post-"
and never "pre-." They help church leaders assess the damage to
past Christendom, but do not help them set foot into the forest
trails in search of Spiritual Redwoods. The maps suddenly end at
the margins, just when church leaders need the most guidance!

In *Sacred Cows Make Gourmet Burgers*, Bill began to explore the
"coastline" of this new age by describing the "quantum world." It
is a world of fluid processes and changing relationships, rather than
fixed forms and enduring structures. In *Kicking Habits: Welcome
Relief for Addicted Churches*, Tom began to explore the "coastline" of
this new age by describing systems of constant change, surrounded by energy fields of core visions, values, and beliefs. Together we
have been further inspired by George Hunter's description of the
new age as a "pre-Christian" world of religious and cultural ferment, and deep and diverse spiritual yearning.

Those thriving Christian organisms described in this book as
"Spiritual Redwoods" have begun to draw a
still more detailed map of the future. They
have realized that the new era is more than
"post-anything." *It is a pre-Christian world!* It is
a world similar to the first century after Jesus.
It is a world of technological change and population migration; a world of systemic injustice
and apocalyptic longing; it is a world of exces-
sive materialism and spiritual yearning; it is a
world of deep anxiety and utter cynicism
toward the religious institutions of the past.

> Spiritual Redwoods are filling in the map to the future.

Here are some of the contrasts already visible in the transition from Christendom to the pre-Christian world that are changing the map for Christians:

Twentieth-Century Christendom	Twenty-First-Century Pre-Christian
Attitudes	
Pendulum Swings	Earthquakes
Ideologies	Intuitions
Ultimate Truths	Dialogical Truths
Provincial Perspectives	Global Perspectives
Metaphors	
Home	Community
Central Fountain	Flood from the Fringe
Inner Warmth	Raging Fire
Evolution	Revolution
Solid	Fluid
Processes	
Either-Or Choices	Both-And Choices
Deductive Analysis	Inductive Synthesis
Input	Output
Male vs. Female Genders	Unique Personhoods
Atomic Thinking	Relational Thinking
Structures	
Formal Boundaries	Changing Patterns
Hierarchy	Organism
Management	Entrepreneurship
Control	Permission
Theology	
Religion	Spirituality
Entitled Offices	Authentic Leaders
Prophetic Confrontation	Visionary Direction
Ethics	Apocalyptics
The Presence of God	The Touch of the Holy

Entitled Offices	Authentic Leaders
Authoritative Voices	Spiritual Coaches
Guardians of Truth	Motivators for Mission

Equipped with a different kind of map, the church leaders and Christian seekers ready to tread the forest paths searching for Spiritual Redwoods also require a basic strategy. It is all too easy to lose one's sense of direction in the forest. There is an ambiguity about every choice. Each path winds through the forest in unexpected ways, and crosses other paths in unexpected places. The spiritual navigation of the twenty-first century relies on four navigational principles.

First, explorers of the forest rely on their *compass*. They continually refer to the core vision that lies at the center of their identity and mission. It is the "True North," to which the compass always turns.

For Moses, it was the Burning Bush. For Isaiah, it was the Cherubim. For Paul, it was the Blinding Light of Christ. For John the Evangelist, it was the New Jerusalem. In the shadows and storms of the forest, nothing looks familiar. Never second-guess your compass, or you will quickly run in circles. The core vision is literally the Song in the Heart explorers of the forest find themselves spontaneously singing as they walk.

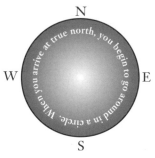

Figure 2.1: Explorers rely on their compass.

Compass Check: Do you find yourself quoting from books more than three years old?

Does your heart quicken when you focus on your core vision?

Is your core vision worth dying for?

Second, explorers of the forest rely on *teamwork*. Air pilots and ship captains already know that during any trip they are off-course 98 percent of the time. Navigation is always a series of course corrections. Therefore, they are in constant communication with the members of the expedition, and with other travelers along the way. Christian explorers of the forest are constantly forming new and creative partnerships with other explorers.

Figure 2.2: Explorers rely on teamwork.

**Figure 2.3: Explorers rely on instinct to recognize
key intersections.**

Teamwork Check: Are you linked with other explorers for support and dialogue?

Does your network cross denominational, cultural, and regional boundaries?

Do you equally value clergy and laity, members and fringe people?

Third, explorers of the forest rely on *instinct*. This intuition, this inner sense of calling, pushes them to look over one more hill. It pushes them to be in a continuous state of learning. It helps them recognize key intersections and choose the right path. It gives them the confidence to take risks and make mistakes, knowing that these are crucial, unavoidable, and necessary for spiritual growth.

Instinct Check: Are you motivated by spiritual curiosity to do more learning? Are you prepared to be wrong? And can you learn from your unavoidable mistakes?

Finally, explorers of the forest rely on *benchmarks*. Benchmarks are the key elevations in the topography of the forest, the intersections of wandering pathways, and the landmarks for key turnings in the road. Benchmarks call the explorers' attention to a moment of significance for their journey, to which they should pay close attention. Benchmarks are spiritual positions from which explorers of the forest can scan the territory in all directions.

Benchmark Check:

"Looking North": Do most newcomers arrive accompanied by lay ministers?
Do the majority of people involved in the church claim no previous connection with the church?
Is the membership of the church smaller than the number of people in worship?

"Looking South": Has cultural, racial, economic, and educational diversity replaced homogeneity in the totality of congregational life?
Is electronic multimedia used routinely by the church for worship, study, and communication?
Has the church abandoned codependent relationships with dysfunctional people to become a legitimate form of ministry?

"Looking East": Is the ministry characterized by enthusiasm for, or embarrassment about, quality?
Is the congregation beyond gender bias?
Do issues of ecology and the environment occupy more and more attention?

"Looking West": Are leaders spending more time among non-Christians than among church members?
Do the personal tastes, lifestyles, and opinions of leaders still define the boundaries of church life and mission?
Is the glue that holds people together consensus, or the continuing experience of the transforming power of Christ?

Church leaders and spiritual seekers enter the forest of the pre-Christian world with a different map, and a distinct strategy of exploration. Down many paths they search. Eventually, the explorer emerges from the confusion of trees to perceive the Spiritual Redwood.

The Church of Philippi: The First "Spiritual Redwood"

The biblical paradigm for the "Spiritual Redwood" is the Gentile church of Philippi. The story of its origin and growth is being repeated over and over on the brink of the twenty-first century.

The mission to the Gentiles drives Spiritual Redwoods.

The "Mission to the Gentiles" was the driving force of Christian ministry in the first century. It was controversial. Established church leaders wanted desperately to conform to historical patterns of Judaic religious practice. They wanted to preserve traditions and maintain a purified heritage. The vision of Peter displacing dietary laws, the conversion of the Godfearer Cornelius (a despised soldier!), and the transformation of the persecutor Saul profoundly shocked the church. The success of the mission to the Gentiles pushed them to crisis. They summoned Paul and Silas back to Jerusalem. In the end, however, the Jerusalem Council wisely decided that all that really mattered was the gospel . . . and nothing else. The church broke out from the limitations of social conformity to become one of the most diverse, magnetic, and adaptive religious movements in history.

The "Mission to the Gentiles" is also the driving force of Christian ministry in the emerging pre-Christian era of the twenty-first century. Once again, the "Gentiles" may broadly be described as "the spiritually yearning, institutionally alienated public." These are the growing numbers of individuals who are fascinated by spirituality, and yet remarkably ignorant of Christianity. They are distrustful of, or even hostile to, institutional churches and organized religion, and yet they yearn to be free, whole, healthy, and connected to a daily walk with the Holy.

The city of Philippi became an important center of Roman culture when veteran soldiers settled there following the battle of Actium. This culturally diverse city of entrepreneurs and seekers would form the first Christian church in Europe; spearhead the spread of Christian faith throughout Greece and the west; contribute enormous sums for the spread of the gospel and the support of the saints; equip and commission missionaries to other parts of the world; and help shape Christian faith and practice for centuries to come.

The story of its birth in Acts 16 provides clues to understanding the growth of this Spiritual Redwood that towered over the tangled cultural forest of the Roman world.

It all begins with Vision. Paul has a vision of a Gentile, a Macedonian, beckoning him to "come over and help us." It is not a Program Committee that has a vision. No Official Board is sent away on retreat, to return with a vision. The vision comes to a single individual, and fills that person's life with new purpose.

This sense of destiny is crucial to the growth of Spiritual Redwoods. Other churches may have more practical resources, or even greater opportunities, but the church with an authentic vision is the only one that can truly thrive. The vision always arises through conversation with, and sensitivity toward, the "Gentiles" of the world. These "Gentiles" are the "spiritually yearning, institutionally alienated public." These are the ones straining for meaning and purpose, longing for freedom and vindication, anxious for spiritual guides who can coach them through the many paths of the forest.

It all endures as Team Vision. Paul shares the vision with Silas, Timothy, and Luke, and together they shape the vision and follow it. What had been a wandering journey down many uncertain paths (16:6-8), suddenly becomes a "straight course" (16:11-12) toward the primary mission field of the day.

This corporate conviction motivates the growth of Spiritual Redwoods today. Their goal is not to take care of institutional insiders, nor is it to perpetuate a glorious denominational heritage. Churches oriented around chaplaincy or survival quickly find themselves wandering in a forest of unclear paths—no matter how large and wealthy they may be. On the other hand, churches prepared to hack their way through the dense forest undergrowth in order to reach out to others will thrive in the twenty-first century—no matter how small or poor they may be.

It all centers on indigenous worship. The second Paul and his ministry team enter Philippi, they seek out a place of prayer. The routine of worship becomes the pivot around which everything else moves.

Worship is held "outside the gate by the river" (16:13). Architectural props are not needed by the Spiritual Redwoods today—only the sustenance of God's transforming, ever-changing grace. The key to worship is that it is an indigenous, flexible, participatory community. It can happen anywhere, anytime, and in any way.

It all builds upon "Midwives." Paul and the ministry team meet Lydia. She is an entrepreneur and a seeker, and she is transformed by the faith-sharing of Paul (16:14). Lydia is incorporated into the team vision, and brings the faith to nurture the individual lives of family, friends, neighbors, work associates, and strangers.

Lydia, and others like her, become the real leadership of Spiritual Redwoods. Their ability to bring transformation to others, to nurture growth in others, and to equip others to fulfill their own destinies in Christ, will be the foundation for the thriving church. Lydia is not an administrator, bureaucrat, fund-raiser, or supervisor. She is a midwife, one who can bring others to birth a new future.

It all grows through Small Groups. The home of Lydia becomes a focus for spiritual growth. Only a few people are needed to begin; "two or three gathered together" in the name of Christ.

Spiritual Redwoods maximize the opportunities for intimacy and personal growth. They are not satisfied with the "mere friendliness" that aims at knowing two hundred people by their first names. They aim at deep, quality relationships that nurture their mutual personal and spiritual growth. Such groups are not committees, councils, or task groups. They are gatherings for discovery and discernment.

It all results in transformations. The story of the healing of the fortune-teller is but one story among many. All Philippi is feeling the impact of personal transformations, which in turn change the whole fabric and behavior of community life. A slave girl is healed of her addiction, and those who profit by the addictions of others are bankrupted (16:16-24).

Spiritual Redwoods encourage radical personal change. Beneath the umbrella of their spreading branches, they inspire changes in values, behavior patterns, lifestyle, beliefs, assumptions, and dreams. People are healed, changed, freed, made different, born anew, given a fresh start, and oriented in a whole new direction. Spiritual Redwoods are not filled with an atmosphere of nostalgia, but with an atmosphere of expectation. What is important is not the past, nor even the present, but the future.

It all shakes the foundations. When the transformations begin to happen, the obstacles emerge. Paul and Silas are arrested, thrown into prison, and fastened in the stocks. They overcome obstacles by returning to their core vision—singing hymns and prayers to God. And God shakes the foundations of the acropolis, setting the prisoners free, and making the jailors into prisoners.

Spiritual Redwoods are always perceived by parent denominations to be iconoclastic and are always perceived by public authorities to be meddlesome and unpredictable. Spiritual Redwoods are always said to be *too "spiritual"* (mystical, fanatical, or enthusiastic), *too "red"* (colorful, extreme, or vivid), or *too "woody"* (involving, big, or intrusive). Like trees growing along a river, they dwarf the bushes that try to grow farther from the water, and may be resented for their size and strength. Like trees planted too close to the foundations of a building, such churches get attention, not because their leaves rustle loudly in the wind, but because their roots quietly pry apart the bricks and mortar of the establishment.

It all leads to enormous diversity. When the prison doors are all opened, not only are the prisoners listening with new ears to the gospel, but jailors are transformed as well. The jailor and his family are baptized. Gathered in the Philippian church are people heretofore enemies or hostile strangers: Lydia and her middle-class family and friends, the slave girl healed from her addictions, a motley collection of former jailbirds, and even their former oppressors (16:33-35).

Spiritual Redwoods harbor an incredible diversity of people within their branches. Homogeneity of membership is not their goal. The basic parameters of church life are not determined by the opinions, values, and lifestyles of a few matriarchs and patriarchs, but by the vision and values and beliefs that arch over the whole church.

Figure 2.4

The bond that holds all this diversity together is not agreement on every issue, nor is it assent to long dogmatic agendas. The bond is nothing more, nor less, than the continuing experience of the transforming power of God that is touching every individual life. **It all demands a tenacity for justice.** The Philippian authorities refuse to take responsibility for their actions, but Paul and Silas insist upon vindication. It is not for themselves only that they act, but for the sake of all that diverse group of vulnerable people who are now the church (16:35-39). No one shall be a victim.

Spiritual Redwoods constantly seek ways to intercede for social justice. However, this is not primarily a matter of petitions to government, or participation in civic committees. These churches combat injustice on a more personal and intimate level, rescuing and supporting individuals who have been victimized in countless ways in today's society. Their real goal is not an altered municipal policy, but an affirmed and redeemed life. **It all requires leaders with the courage to get out of the way.** Finally, Paul and the ministry team that began it all do an amazing thing. They leave. They equip Lydia and her associates for excellence, and then they move on, move over, get out of the way (16:40).

> Spiritual Redwoods defy definition, but you know one when you see it.

Leadership of a Spiritual Redwood is all about letting go of control. The organization does not tell people what to do, but helps people discern their callings themselves, and then equips them to pursue those callings with excellence. People who have a need to control, or a need to be controlled—people who love to hold offices, or who cannot act without permission from authoritative offices—will be uncomfortable in such a thriving church. These churches are all about risking and learning, laughing and experimenting, letting loose the energies of God's people to give birth to new life.

In a sense, "Spiritual Redwoods" defy definition. They are more of an art form than a mission statement. They are larger than life, with an almost mythic power.

- They stand taller than any other tree, but their visibility is less a function of the numbers of their adherents, and more the magnitude of their ministries.

- They hold aloft an enormous umbrella of intertwined branches, which shelter a huge diversity of life in an atmosphere of peace and mutual respect.
- They are resistant to crisis from beyond and disease from within. Political winds do not break them, and ideological fires cannot burn them.
- They put down strong, extensive root systems that intertwine with those of other Redwoods. They draw nutrition from unexpected sources, and reach out into unlikely places.
- They regenerate in abundance. Not only do seeds initiate new life across the forest floor, but they sprout vigorously even from the stumps of felled trees.

The "Spiritual Redwood" may defy complete description, but spiritual explorers of the twenty-first century know one when they see it.

VISTA THREE

Beneath, Behind, and Beyond

Jesus the Heartwood of Spiritual Redwoods

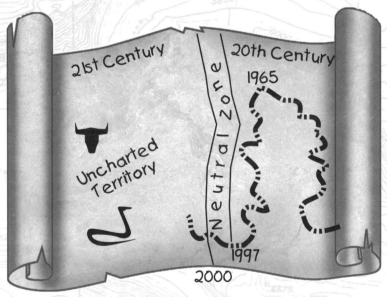

21st Century

Uncharted
Territory

Neutral zone

20th Century

1965

1997

2000

The most
important step to
finding the right direction
is to fall in love with Jesus.

T *he forest is a constant conversation. The birds call, the insects hum, the branches of the bushes crackle, and the leaves of the trees rustle with the wind . . . and all together communicate each changing nuance of the environment. Animals signal to each other discoveries of food, opportunities for shelter, warnings of danger, and invitations for companionship. Botanists have discovered that even the trees can communicate with one another, issuing warnings of disease that allow others of their species to prepare a defense. Philosophers demonstrate that the removal of a single stone, or the erosion of a single hill, affects the lives of every entity of the forest in ripples of significance. Everything is in relation. Everything is in process.*

Not even the giant Redwood can survive without participating in the constant conversation of the forest. It cannot grow in isolation from the forest, nor can it grow in confrontation with the forest, but only in conversation with the forest. The Redwood can live hundreds of years. It can survive many seeming disasters. It can change, grow, and evolve in many unique ways. Yet all this health and vitality will only be possible if the Redwood remains sensitive and responsive to the nuances of the environment experienced by even the smallest—even the most "unimportant"—of God's creations.

Beneath, behind, and beyond the forest itself lies a deeper mystery. It is the Power of Life and the Meaning of Life. It is "The Holy." Augustine described it as a perfect unity of Agape and Eros. Rudolf Otto described it as "Mysterium Tremendum." Paul Tillich described it as "Power of Being and Ground of Being." Charles Wesley celebrated it as "Depth of Mercy," and "Love divine, all loves excelling." It is a Holiness that can both sustain the forest and rend the forest. It is manifest in both seed and tornado, water and fire. The Redwood can be its vehicle, but can never contain its fullness.

The greatest tragedy of the forest is despair. It arises from alienation from the forest's Ground of Being, or separation from the Holy. Despair is a bankruptcy of meaning, and an utter absence of hope. It is the entrapment of a creature in habitually self-destructive behavior patterns that are chronically denied, and yet which lead the creature to contradict its own destiny. Release and rescue will not come from the effort or intelligence of the creature, but only through the intervention of a Higher Power, the Transforming Power of God, that is the deeper mystery of the forest.

Churches that aspire to grow as "Spiritual Redwoods" participate in the conversation of the community. They are attuned to human culture and natural environment. They know that spirituality, cultural forms, and environmental realities are all interrelated and ever changing. Anyone and anything can be a vehicle for the expression of God—but never contain the fullness of God. Therefore, the church recognizes that God will simultaneously employ and shatter all programs, all doctrines, all ideologies, all structures, and all offices . . . even within the church itself. The church knows that all that really matters is the gospel, the "welcome relief" of the depth of mercy and love divine that is the essence of the Holy.

The single most important reality surrounding conversation about God for the twenty-first century is *where*, and *with whom*, and *to what purpose* that conversation is taking place. Consider the following story, which is being repeated countless times on a daily and hourly basis in North America:

A few months ago, Tom was on his way to a meeting outside one of the fastest growing cities in North America. It was evening, he was late (as usual), and he hadn't taken time for supper. He stopped at random, where restaurants line the highway.

The restaurant he chose was not very busy. They seated everyone together near the front windows to give the appearance of popularity. As he was seated, he noticed two men at the adjacent table. Judging by the sample cases on the floor, and the suit coats hanging from the backs of the chairs, he guessed they were salesmen relaxing together after a busy day of work.

They had long ago finished their meal, and sat with coffee cups before them. It was clear that they were rapt in intense conversation. The waitress who refilled their cups went unnoticed. Throughout Tom's entire dinner, they talked and talked, with frequent animation. One man began to speak the most, and the other listened with such an expression of eagerness that one just had to eavesdrop!

The one man was sharing with his colleague the "bottom-line" reason that he did not commit suicide. He was persuading his partner not to despair, and listing the real reasons he thought it was worthwhile to give the world one more day. He talked about Jesus, not with any vast knowledge of biblical quotations or historical doctrines, but simply from his own daily experience of the transforming power of God. *And his friend was drinking it in with his coffee!*

Before they left the restaurant, the Christian had invited the pre-Christian to worship with him in his church. Now, Tom knew of this church. Some of the members of that church were controversial. Some of the worship services of that church used music with less than the best aesthetic qualities. Some of their ideas were strange, and some of their activities seemed a little crazy. Yet somehow none of that really mattered now. Suddenly it wasn't too hard to understand why this church was one of the most dynamic and diverse churches in North America.

Such experiences are not rare. In fact, they happen far more frequently than most "Church Folks" want to admit. When such experiences are reported, "Church Folks" are incredulous. *"When? Where? I've never overheard such conversations!"* It is as if "Church Folks" are tuned into the wrong radio frequency, in the mistaken belief that it is the only radio frequency. As they listen to the wrong signals, a continuous and diverse cultural conversation about Christianity is happening in which the institutional church does not participate.

In order to find the right frequency, "Church Folks" need to "adjust their sets" by making three crucial distinctions. The first distinction is that people do not want to talk about religion; *they do want to talk about spirituality!* There is no doubt that the term "spirituality" has been overworked and underdefined, but there is also no doubt that ordinary people are talking about "spiritual experience" with an interest, enthusiasm, and passion that has not been seen in North America for a long, long time. The distinction may jar, annoy, or frustrate "Church Folks." The religion "Church Folks" want to discuss is a body of correct information and acceptable behavior with which they want others to agree and conform. The "spirituality" about which people want to talk is an attitude or orientation to daily living, and perspective from anyone is equally welcome.

The second distinction is that people do not want to listen to professional experts; *they do want to learn from spiritual travelers!* Such spiritual travelers are not certified experts and knowledgeable academics, nor are they charismatic gurus and cultic dictators. They are simply people who have "been there, done that, and grown because of it," who are now "going somewhere, doing things, and moving forward," and who are kind enough to spend time to help others along the way. They do not merely speak from experience. They speak from experiences which they themselves have personally questioned, challenged, interpreted, and survived.

The third distinction is that people do not want to talk about divine abstractions; *they do want to talk about Jesus!* The public is no longer satisfied with mere "God Talk." Fewer and fewer people are interested in stories about "the Creator God and Slow Growth," or in explanations of the "First Cause and Universal Orderliness." Such a God is too distant, and they frankly don't have the time to grow slowly in an era when the world seems to be going to ruin and a new generation of technology appears every three months. Similarly, fewer and fewer people are interested in disembodied spirits that guide people on endless treks through troubled times. They are just too frustrated and exhausted by the complexity and intensity of daily life. No, the focus of conversation on the brink of the twenty-first century is quite specifically on the transforming power of God. For Christians, this means the conversation must be about Jesus. He is the one associated with transformations, transfigurations, and healings. The public is passionately interested in being transformed and changed—by a God who can touch and be touched—on a daily basis.

One might say that there is a resurgent interest in "Christology" amid the cultural conversation about spirituality and personal change. However, institutional "Church Folks" have difficulty perceiving it, understanding it, or participating in it, because this conversation about Jesus has rejected the accumulated christological terminology of the institutional church. Indeed, even the term "Christ" carries little meaning.

> Too many "Church Folk" just don't get it ...yet.

One Christian leader in a growing rural-suburban community in Ontario reports that participation by educated, spiritually seeking, institutionally alienated adults is growing. She understands herself to be a spiritual "midwife" in conversation with others about the transforming power of God. One of her chief concerns is to convince seekers that it is inappropriate for "recreational" drug abusers to be teachers of children in the Christian education program. "When I speak of Christ," she says, "their eyes glaze and they fidget uncomfortably. But when I speak of Jesus, they are all attention!"

The term "Christ" carries an enormous weight of complex dogma, and invites seekers into an arena of religious disagreement and institutional obligation that is (to them) frightening in its irrelevance. In the same way, terms like "Lord," "Messiah," "King," "Son of God," and even "Savior" have become so laden with underlying nuances that seekers are too nervous to consider them. The use of such terms requires a greater theological knowledge than most people possess, and a deeper commitment to institutional church tradition than most people want. Such terms have become relics of a Christendom that has passed away.

The Church in Conversation with Itself: What Is Disappearing

The contribution of the church to the growing cultural conversation about Jesus has sometimes been in response to the genuine spiritual yearnings of people, and sometimes happened simply to preserve its own institutional agendas. As the spiritual yearnings of the public have changed, and as the public became increasingly alienated from institutional religious agendas, churches have found themselves only minor voices in the larger cultural conversation about Jesus. They find they can only talk about Jesus *if the context of the conversation is their own doctrinal agenda about Christ*, and that they spend most of their time with the public *first trying to persuade people to accept the institutional agenda of their church*. They are not, strictly speaking, in a *conversation* at all! Their purpose is to edify and correct, rather than to listen and learn. The ideological and theological agenda of the church comes first, and talk about Jesus is intended to follow from it. Yet the public no longer has any patience with the theological and ideological agendas of the institutional church—and talk about Jesus never happens.

One might say that, on the brink of the twenty-first century, "Church Folks" have a remarkably small "market share" of the "Jesus Talk" happening among the public. It is not that "Church Folks" disagree with the "Jesus Talk" going on around them;

"Church Folks" have a remarkably small "market share" of the "Jesus Talk."

they just don't hear it. They just don't get it. They just can't connect with it.

At the conclusion of a consultation in a local church, the pastor drove Bill to the airport. The event had been a friendly, but rather frustrating experience. In the midst of the idle conversation, the pastor paused, looked at Bill with a puzzled expression, and said, "During the seminar you mentioned several times the need for people to have a personal relationship with Jesus. What on earth did you mean by that?"

The images of Christ which have been dear to institutional churches, and over which institutional churches have quarreled with great passion, hold less and less interest for the spiritually yearning masses. Three images of Christ are disappearing.

The Utopian Christ and the Dream of an Achievable, Just Society

The intense civil, national, legal, and economic unrest of the last twenty years has turned the idealistic "baby boomers" of North America cynical. A whole generation of church leaders who grew up singing "If I Had a Hammer" and "They'll Know We Are Christians by Our Love," have subsequently left the professional ministry for other careers, or are experiencing various degrees of psychological burnout. They have painfully discovered that they could hammer all morning and all evening, but by the end of the week things seemed worse than ever.

The subsequent generation of "baby busters," of course, never believed that a uniformly just society was achievable anyway. Life never was fair for them, but only ironic, and therefore it must be lived with a hearty and irreverent sense of humor that serious social reformers and pious "Church Folks" find most annoying. They will go out of their way to befriend the refugee family across the street, but joining a political movement to restructure society is a waste of time.

The Utopian Christ is disappearing from cultural conversation about God. This is not to say that people no longer care about justice, nor does it imply that God does not care about justice. It means that the image of Christ as the example and inspiration for social reform through political organization and parliamentary procedure is becoming irrelevant. The Christ who was the divine companion of the picket line has been revealed to be remarkably impotent to move beyond rhetoric and bring lasting change. The Christ who would reign over a just society through better education, more effective communication, universal health care, and proper social management has been revealed to be a *mere ideology* at best, and *tragic idolatry* at worst.

The Ecclesiastical Christ and the Dream of a Doctrinally Consistent Christology

The growing disenchantment with institutions in general, and the institution of the church in particular, has led North Americans to an important discovery about Christian doctrine. They do not understand it. They do not want to understand it. But most important—and here is the key discovery at the end of the twentieth century—*they do not need to understand it!* Understanding the saving grace of God in a rationally consistent, historically grounded way is not important to most North Americans. *Experiencing* that saving grace in ways that personally transform one's life is everything.

North Americans are among the best educated and best informed people in the world, but they have discovered that rational understanding is overrated. Professionals with advanced degrees command immense knowledge, and yet are in no better position to overcome their destructive addictions than the least educated. Veteran "Church Folk" can understand the complexities of the Trinity, and yet are helpless to assist their own children to appreciate and love God. The equation between "Truth" and "Doctrinal Competence" has broken down. "Truth" for the twenty-first century is a power that changes the heart.

The Ecclesiastical Christ is also disappearing from public conversation about God. This is not to say that interpreting one's experience of salvation with integrity is unimportant. It means that the experience of grace precedes the understanding of grace, and that integrity of interpretation is no longer measured by continuity with the historical record.

"Truth" for the twenty-first century is a power that changes the heart.

A dying congregation decided to do a lay witness mission in hope of "jump-starting" congregational renewal. Attendance reached an all-time high. Many people felt God's presence through the faith-stories shared by lay witnesses. Still other people later testified that their lives were transformed. Nevertheless, when the pastor was asked what he thought about it, he responded: "The theology was awful. It will take me years to straighten them out!" Congregational renewal perished . . . and the congregation continued to die.

The institutional church—and the certified "officials" of that church—are no longer decisive voices influencing each person's unique perspective on Christ. The Christ who would critique every individual's experience of the Holy, and reign supreme over a consistent orthodoxy of public agreement, has been revealed to be *mere heritage* at best . . . and tragic idolatry at worst.

The Magical Christ and the Dream of Eternal, Personal Safety

Notwithstanding continued notices in the personal columns and want ads of local community newspapers praising the Holy Spirit, the public has grown cynical about divine power. Too many examples of gratuitous evil have assaulted their life experience. The innocent are injured, the pure are struck down by disease, and ordinary neighbors and fellow citizens are abused and hurt by random "crazy people." The drive-by shooting has become a symbol for the inevitable vulnerability and insecurity that characterizes modern experience, whether urban, suburban, rural, or remote.

More than this, the promise of eternal, personal security *in heaven* is also being greeted by growing public indifference. We no longer live in a segmented society. Our relationships are everything. The well-being of my intimates, my family members, my neighbors, and indeed, even nameless sufferers who have become personal acquaintances through the power of television, shares equal importance with my personal survival. Even the well-being of the animals, the trees, the stones, and the ozone layer matter to the modern person as much as does personal safety. The promise of personal, eternal security has become empty, so long as the relationships we cherish cannot be included.

The Magical Christ is disappearing from public conversation. This is not to say that people do not continue to yearn for an inbreaking of grace that might even circumvent the laws of nature. It means that "licking the boots" of Deity—through chanting the right liturgies, joining the right religious associations, or speaking the politically correct vocabulary—cannot manipulate God to do what we want. It means that "Want-Ad Religion" is not a long-term answer to suicide. The Christ who would guarantee personal security has been revealed to be a *mere human neurosis.*

These three images of Christ have largely shaped the bitter disputes that have preoccupied Christendom, especially in the latter half of the twentieth century. Some picture a "Prophetic Christ," who is both moral example and ethical motivator for social justice. Others insist on a "Transcendent Christ," who is continuous with the historical definitions of the church and who saves people from sin. And still others argue for a "Personal Christ," who rewards complete self-surrender with assistance in scoring well on examinations, winning athletic competitions, and preventing divorce or disease.

Polarizations between "liberals" and "conservatives," or between "personalists" and "traditionalists," have divided congregations and fractured denominations. Yet with the collapse of Christendom, the spiritual conversation of North American culture has left all three christological images behind. In the emerging pre-Christian era, these have more to do with ideology and ecclesiology than authentic faith.

The *real, authentic,* and *vibrant* conversation about the fullness of Christ is happening not inside the church, but beyond the church. And it is happening all the time, everywhere, in restaurants, fast-food diners, sports arenas, city parks, neighborhood parties, school playgrounds, and anywhere else the public gathers. Those church leaders and congregations who persist in arguing old polarities and historical trivialities will be pushed to the extreme margins of religious life in North America. Those church leaders and congregations who choose to sit in on that conversation are becoming the "Spiritual Redwoods" of the emerging pre-Christian era.

The Church in Conversation with Culture: What Is Emerging

Spiritual Yearnings are different from mere dreams. They do not derive from the wishful thinking of an institutional agenda, but arise from the suffering and frustration of individual experience. Dreams rocket across the horizon of culture like shooting stars— compelling, but brief. Spiritual Yearnings are the deep-down aches of the heart that persist in and pervade daily life. These are what really drive human behavior. They are the bedrock of biblical visions. Dreams appear to be very specific, detailed, and concrete—but then expect reality to change so that they might be born. Yearnings are often vague and ill-defined, but they allow visions to shape themselves in unexpected ways. Frustrated Dreamers say, "If only you would word your question differently, then I would have the perfect answer!" Satisfied Yearning sighs, "This is what I needed all along, and never knew it!"

The Apocalyptic Jesus and the Spiritual Yearning to Be Changed

"Zacchaeus, hurry and come down; for I must stay at your house today" (Luke 19:5). With these words, the Apocalyptic Jesus who turns the world upside down and inside out, addresses the spiritual yearning of the twenty-first-century public. Like Zacchaeus, they are "tax collectors" (capitalists, materialists, business men and women, upwardly mobile and inwardly shallow, more comfortable in shopping malls than in worship centers). Like Zacchaeus, they are climbing every available "sycamore tree" (religious experience, New Age trend, or self-help book) to catch a glimpse of meaningful living. They yearn to change. Beset by backbreaking routines, insensitive corporate bosses, loveless marriages, and pointless vacations, they yearn to be different. They yearn to be transformed into something else. Jesus does what even "virtual reality" video games cannot do. Jesus comes to stay—in their home—transforms their "rat race" into meaningful existence.

The Apocalyptic Jesus is simultaneously a frightening surprise and a welcome relief, and it is impossible to separate one reaction from the other. Change means "death" and "birth," and it is never clear whether the immediate tears are of pain or joy. The Apocalyptic Jesus does not so much respond to human need, as suddenly seize upon human desperation to rip the evil out of life. Dinner with the Apocalyptic Jesus probably left Zacchaeus happier and more content, but it also left him at least temporarily unemployed and unpopular.

This Apocalyptic Jesus changes more than individual lives. Since every life is perceived today to be interconnected with every other life, what changes is the world itself. This is not a matter of political agitation or better education. Transformation progresses in a kind of explosive chain reaction. It does not become a part of my life. Instead, I become a part of its life. The yearning to be changed, to be different, is a yearning for ecstasy, to literally "stand beyond oneself" and to be "carried away" in a movement of grace that transforms everything and everyone—even, in the end, "the least" of Jesus' brothers and sisters.

The Healing Jesus and the Spiritual Yearning to Be Whole

"Someone touched me; for I noticed that power had gone out from me" (Luke 8:46). With these words, the Healing Jesus whose touch brings health and wholeness to diseased and broken people, addresses the spiritual yearning of the twenty first-century public. Like this woman hemophiliac, the public has spent all its money in doctors' fees, in the midst of failing national health-care systems and rising hospital costs. They are hurting in any number of physical, emotional, or mental ways, having fallen through gaping holes in Medicare, Social Security, and the social safety net. They are surrounded and pursued by broken relationships and unresolved grief. Like this woman, they are reaching out to touch and be touched.

The Healing Jesus is directly accessible. No membership in a community of faith is required. No liturgies, biblical knowledge, or doctrinal consensus is necessary. No designated "sacred space" is important. The healing may happen by the roadside, in commuter traffic, at a rock concert, in the coffee shop—or pop culture restaurants like TGI Friday's. The yearning alone is sufficient, and the boldness that risks reaching out to Christ. In the twenty-first century, yearning and boldness equal faith.

The Healing Jesus is first and foremost a healer of *persons*, not of society or nations or ecclesiastical institutions. This is not a metaphorical healing, but a quite literal, deeply personal, and sometimes miraculous healing. Nevertheless, the *healing of persons* leads to the *wholeness of peoples*. In a sense, the Healing Jesus creates "healers." The former madman Legion returns home, to "declare how much God has done" for him (Luke 8:39). The woman who touches Jesus' robe not only is made well, but walks in peace.

The Addiction-Free Jesus and the Spiritual Yearning to Be Free

"Unbind him, and let him go" (John 11:44). With these words, the Addiction-Free Jesus, who is absolutely unfettered by any habitually destructive behavior patterns, addresses the spiritual yearnings of the twenty-first-century public. Like Lazarus and his sisters, they are trapped by addictions: codependent relationships, alcohol and drug abuse, sexual promiscuity, materialism, work, and any number of other debilitating habits as yet unnamed. Modern people may have no sense of sin, but they know very well the meaning of addiction. It is a bondage which cannot be escaped by human knowledge or effort, and it is inevitable death.

Authenticity is the only grounds for authority.

The Addiction-Free Jesus has an authenticity which is unique in all the world. Using the metaphors of Paul, the Addiction-Free Jesus is like a "New Adam," the epitome of every man or woman, the very essence of humanity . . . but with all the corruptibility removed. Among the twenty-first-century public, authenticity is the *only* grounds for authority. Office-holding, titles, and bureaucratic status mean nothing. Authenticity is everything. Only the Addiction-Free Jesus can have power over addiction. When Paul complains that "I do not do the good I want, but the evil I do not want is what I do," he simply repeats the lament of the addicted public. Who will save us from "this body of death"? The Addiction-Free Jesus.

Freedom from addiction is the primary context for conversation about resurrection in the twenty-first century. The biblical texts that are now merely nostalgic in the funeral home, carry power beyond imagination in the donut shops and sports arenas of the community. Drugs and other addictions are the new tombstones of the twenty-first century that need to be rolled away, and it is in response to this yearning to be free that Jesus says *"I am the resurrection and the life."*

The Equipping Jesus and the Spiritual Yearning for Mentors

"With many such parables [Jesus] spoke the word . . . but he explained everything in private to his disciples" (Mark 4:33, 34). Jesus spent most of his time with just twelve people. He teaches them to pray (Luke 11:1), resolves their numerous quarrels and misgivings (Mark 9:33), takes them away on retreat (John 6:3), washes their feet (John 13), and sends them on "work-study" missions that combine action and reflection (Matt. 11:1). He spends large amounts of time equipping twelve people to live lives of value and meaning.

This Equipping Jesus addresses the spiritual yearning of the twenty-first-century public. They are desperately searching for "mentors" (or "midwives"). Such people are authentic, vulnerable, wise, and compassionate. They are able to bond spiritually and personally with others, helping the other to endure and interpret ambiguity. Mentors and midwives can confirm and celebrate healing, and guide others to move beyond healing to real helping. Mentors and midwives are not mere enablers, because they are dedicated to their own mission, and the needs of even the closest disciple will not distract them from their quest. Yet they elicit from others their own sense of destiny.

The Equipping Jesus is the eternal, daily spiritual guide. Jesus appears to the disciples on the road to Emmaus (Luke 24:13-35) to interpret Scripture and renew hope. Jesus counsels the transformed to live in ambiguities, trains the healed to help others, and coaches former addicts to live "one day at a time." Jesus comes across the stormy sea, enters the sinking boat, and announces *"It is I; do not be afraid"* (John 6:20).

The Advocate Jesus and the Spiritual Yearning for Vindication

"Let anyone among you who is without sin be the first to throw a stone" (John 8:7). With these words, the Advocate Jesus who defends the helpless and challenges the self-righteous, addresses the spiritual yearning of the twenty-first-century public. Like the woman accused of adultery, they yearn for a second chance. Some may not *feel* guilty; some may not *be* guilty; and others sense that the punishments they receive are incommensurate with the wrongs

they have done. In the complexities and power struggles of the twenty-first century, everyone feels victimized.

The Advocate Jesus stands with victims. His power not only works *internally*, to raise hope and self-esteem, but also *externally*, to challenge self-righteousness and justice that has been corrupted by its own smugness. Jesus is perpetually finding value within the most evil people and is constantly vindicating persons. Whether it means walking a second mile, surrendering a coat, or turning the cheek, the Advocate Jesus is always giving people another chance.

The Advocate Jesus walks with victims. His power not only works *individually*, to build safe relationships and intimate trust, but also *corporately*, to confront racism, sexism, and all the other systemic ways groups victimize other groups. Jesus is perpetually equalizing society toward the highest common denominator, and liberating talent to fulfill its potential. Whether it means overturning the tables of the financial establishment, harvesting illegal corn in order to feed the hungry, or inviting outcasts to sit in places of honor at the national table, the Advocate Jesus is always giving people*s* another chance.

Escape from victimization is the primary context of conversation about justice in the twenty-first century. Biblical texts which have become mere rhetoric in the political arena carry power beyond imagination among those who have been institutionalized or who are in regular therapies for stress relief. The Advocate Jesus brings people to an awareness of their conscious or unconscious complicity with evil . . . and to an awareness of their self-worth and opportunity for self-transcendence. The Advocate Jesus assaults the processes of victimization, whether illegal or legal, and lobbies perpetually for a second chance. *"Go your way, and from now on do not sin again."*

Jesus, the Heir to Eden, and the Spiritual Yearning for a Personally Meaningful Destiny

"I am the true vine. . . . Those who abide in me and I in them bear much fruit, because apart from me you can do nothing" (John 15:1, 5). With these words, the New Adam who would restore Creation to original purity, simultaneously addresses the two central yearnings of the twenty-first-century public for the "End of Time." First, the public has discovered that true fulfillment does not come from

eternal retired bliss, but from meaningful, purposeful activity. They yearn to play an indispensable role in a movement of divine proportions. The magnetism of Jesus is the promise that in relationship with the Heir to Eden people can be incredibly productive for lasting goodness. Second, the public intuitively knows that the interrelational world in which they live will avoid being a deadly trap only if the organism of Life itself grows and evolves. It is a vine, a plant, that must grow to live. The vision that grips public imagination is that organic growth and unity with Jesus belong together.

The urgency and passion to rescue the environment is most powerfully motivated by the vision to recover the perfection of the original creation. Authentic sensuality is making a religious "comeback" in the twenty-first century. The goal is not just to create a cleaner world for our children, but also to recover an eternal harmony that is the true destiny of humankind. Such a yearning fuels the struggle for clean water, or the energy to pick up cans beside the roadways of North America. The abiding presence of the Heir to Eden converts a Utopian dream into an authentic quest.

Paul the apostle captures this yearning for the first century: *"We know that the whole creation has been groaning in labor pains [and] waits with eager longing for the revealing of the children of God"* (Rom. 8:22, 19). His metaphor of Jesus as the New Adam who can lead the return to Eden, in response to the crisis of the Old Adam who was expelled from Eden, speaks powerfully to the twenty-first-century public. When he writes that *"the sufferings of this present time are not worth comparing with the glory about to be revealed"* (Rom. 8:18), he echoes the encouragement of the Heir to Eden in promising *"that my joy may be in you, and that your joy may be complete"* (John 15:11). In the twenty-first century, duty motivates nothing. Joy motivates everything.

Representing Jesus in a Pre-Christian World

The pre-Christian world of the twenty-first century is a complex, ambiguous world, in which addiction is the number-one health issue and victimization is the universal experience. In such a world the transforming power of God excites everyone's interest. Jesus attracts widespread attention. Churches that help people experience relationship with Jesus become havens of clarity and safety amid the tangled forest.

It is becoming ever more clear that those churches emerging as "Spiritual Redwoods" in the forest of North American culture emphasize Jesus, and one's relationship with Jesus, as the fundamental issue of faith and purposeful living. *At the same time, however, these churches celebrate enormous diversity of perspective about Jesus, and enormous variety in the manner in which people find themselves "in relationship" with Jesus.*

These churches clearly articulate in their conversation with North American culture their answer to the key question for ministry in the twenty-first century: *What is it about our experience with Jesus that this community cannot live without?*

What is it about our *experience*—
not our dogma or doctrine, not our historical knowledge,
not our reasoned opinion—
but what is it about our heartfelt, practical, and daily *experience* of
    Jesus, that continually and radically changes, modifies,
    improves, and redirects the course of our daily living?
Moreover, what is it about this *experience* of Jesus,
that is so unique, precious, and universally significant,
that unless we share it with someone else,
their lives will be impoverished and lacking—
but if we do share it with someone else,
their lives will be immeasurably enriched?

Their "answer" to this question may not be a statement, but a song. It may not be an essay, but a picture. It may not be offered in prose or in preaching, but in poetry and in dancing. Jesus, and our relationship with Jesus, is the very root and foundation of the church which aspires to grow into a Spiritual Redwood. Yet this experience of Jesus may not be systematically stated in words. Jesus, and our relationship with Jesus, always defy complete definition and explanation.

It is the relationship with Jesus, to which all metaphors point, that is their primary concern. Jesus is more than a historic figure, more than a wise teacher, more than a moral example, and more than a miracle worker. Jesus is the transforming power of God. Jesus is "the fullness of God" in purposeful and timely connection with every creature great or small. Jesus is the "Meaning-Giver" and the "Hope-Bringer" who reconciles all things in heaven and on earth (Col. 1:19-20).

Churches that aspire to be Spiritual Redwoods are centered on Jesus, and yet their roots are not entwined around a single rational explanation of the meaning of Jesus. Their root systems span many perspectives, and draw sustenance from many symbols. Church participants may find meaning from different metaphors, or themselves discover new metaphors as time and experience shape their individual needs and hopes. The Christology of the church is more "collage" than "snapshot," because it continually points to a mystery beyond itself.

The extraordinary combination of the absolute centrality of Jesus, with enormous variety of perspective about Jesus, makes the Spiritual Redwoods of the new age a radically different kind of church. Two great questions challenge the emerging church of the twenty-first century concerning their representation of Jesus in the pre-Christian era.

First, *What is our point of continuity with the historical experience of Christians with Jesus?* Christendom may have ended, but the unfolding story of human beings in relationship to Jesus has not. There must be a continuity between our experience with Jesus today, and the experience of people with Jesus over time. A new era in Christianity may be emerging, but it is Christianity nonetheless. There have been other dramatic changes in Christian history: the schism between the Eastern and Western churches, the Reformation and Renaissance, the Enlightenment, and the rise of denominationalism, to name some of the most significant. In the midst of traumatic historical change, elements of continuity with the experience of Christians with Jesus give integrity and direction for the future.

Incarnational theology is the "heartwood" of the Spiritual Redwood. Their experience with Jesus is the immediacy of the fullness of God. It is simultaneously embraceable and elusive. Participants in the Spiritual Redwood are powerfully motivated to share their experience of Jesus with others, and yet can never quite adequately articulate that experience in words. Never has the divine been more "real," and never has the divine been more "mysterious."

Perhaps it is no surprise, then, that Spiritual Redwoods will find their point of continuity with the past in the first flowering of incarnational theology. In the first pre-Christian era, as in the newly emerging pre-Christian era, there were many perspectives on the person and work of Jesus. Controversies became both bitter and complex. Christians lamented the loss of simplicity and harmony on the one hand, and the multiplication of baffling formulas and endless theological jargon on the other. Finally, the Council of Chalcedon of A.D. 451 sought to end the intolerance and bickering by identifying this single, essential truth:

> that Jesus was at once both fully God and fully Human,
> and that this unique paradox, irrational though it might be,
> is the only essential mystery of faith necessary for salvation.

In a sense, the Council resolved conflict about the person and work of Jesus by declaring that every perspective was both right and wrong. The truth of Jesus could be described with many metaphors, and the benefits of relationship with Jesus could be experienced in many forms, but the whole truth about Jesus lay forever beyond human imagination and inquiry.

Spiritual Redwoods of the new pre-Christian era do what their ancestors in Chalcedon tried to accomplish at the close of the first pre-Christian era. They have emerged from similar conflicts, and celebrate a similar point of view. They are "incarnational" churches in which the central mystery of Jesus as fully God (perfectly loving, wise, and powerful) and fully Human (vulnerable to suffering, empathically compassionate, personally touched and touchable) lies at the heart of their experience of salvation. The cross and resurrection of Jesus do not necessarily imply any particular theory or explanation of atonement, but simply guarantee that this central mystery of Jesus that *was* true, also *remains true for eternity*. Like the branch grafted onto the True Vine, what is crucial is that an indi-

Incarnational theology is the "heartwood" of the Spiritual Redwood.

vidual "participate in" or "be in relationship with" this mysterious Jesus. Spiritual Redwoods of our pre-Christian era are not primarily an "Easter People." They are primarily a "Christmas People"! This mystery, this paradox, is all that really matters. Everything else is metaphor. Everything else is valuable perspective, but always discussable, debatable, and changeable. This paradox of incarnation is the thread of continuity between all representations of Jesus, and the reality of personal experience with Jesus. It is the thread of continuity that ties all the imperfect and imprecise spiritual yearnings of the cultural forest together, for it is the mystery that lies behind life itself. It is the thread of continuity between the people called "Christian" today, and the people called "Christian" yesterday.

Second, *How can we celebrate Jesus . . . and avoid religious bigotry?* The absolute centrality of Jesus for Spiritual Redwoods of our pre-Christian era raises a specter of religious bigotry that can be alarming in our profoundly multicultural and interfaith world. Resolution of this question will increasingly become the greatest challenge for these new churches. Fortunately, the very continuity between the experience of Christians with Jesus today and in the past, previously described, provides direction for a solution.

Consider the following story from Tom's pastoral experience, that is being repeated in countless ways across North America— the greatest Mission Field of the world today.

Islam is one of the fastest growing religions in North America, encouraged not only by immigration, but by the desire of many North American subcultures to find an alternative moral vitality. There are mosques in the heat of Miami, and mosques among the mining towns of northern Canada.

As a pastor in one city, I befriended the local Sunni Imam (leader of the Muslim community in that region). Intelligent, quiet, compassionate, and deeply spiritual, he was a natural conversation partner. The fact that his Muslim community, and my Christian community, seemed to cross programming paths so often surprised both of us and piqued our interest.

We would meet periodically in the little coffee shop across the street. As our friendship and mutual respect grew, we discovered two important things.

"You know," he said to me, "the truth is that I cannot talk more than two minutes about God without talking about

Koran. Koran is more than a book for us . . . it is the very power of God that changes and sustains true believers." "I understand this," I replied with new insight. "I cannot talk about God for more than two minutes without talking about Jesus. Jesus is more than a historical figure for us . . . Jesus is the transforming power of God that changes people."

The other discovery we made was that during our conversation about Koran and Christ, conversation in the coffee shop had suddenly ceased. People were eavesdropping. They were listening. Some would talk with him further. Some would talk with me further. To those who talked to my Muslim friend, I said, "God bless you!" . . . and to those who talked to me he said, "May Allah light your path!" He and I disagree about many things . . . but we share something far more fundamental.

This story is not merely an illustration of religious tolerance. It is an illustration of profound interfaith conversation that is in fact *encouraged* by the central paradox of Christian faith celebrated by Spiritual Redwoods of the new era.

Only the mysterious paradox of incarnation is essential to Christian faith. All else is metaphor. And yet there is an urgency to the metaphors! The transforming experience of companionship with Jesus invites, encourages, even *demands* telling and describing. People must tell their stories, make sense of their lives, and strive to understand God's purposes. The mystery of incarnation inspires a veritable riot of definition, description, and perspective. It proves to be a celebration of diversity in the cultural forest of our times.

The same mystery that is the thread of continuity between experience and description, also guides the Spiritual Redwood to avoid dogmatism, intolerance, and religious bigotry.

First, the whole truth about Jesus is a mystery. The paradox of Jesus as fully God and fully Human is an authentic paradox. It is irrational, and defies explanation. There is no comprehensive statement, confession, or creed to which one can give assent that can possibly "say it all." Such a paradox invites diversity—indeed, welcomes diversity!—both within and beyond the church. Conversation allows the Christian not only to share, but to learn.

Second, relationship with Jesus is experiential. The experience of the transforming power of God precedes any rational statement of faith, and acceptance of some stated dogma does not function as a gate through which one must pass to gain access to that grace. Relationship with Jesus is a matter not of intellectual conversion and agreement with correct propositional statements, but of personal transformation and evidence of a change in behavior. Wherever personal transformation occurs, in whatever form and in whatever context, there is an opportunity to discern Jesus. Therefore, the point of interfaith conversation is not to decide which religious propositions are right or wrong, but to build connections between one's own experience of the divine and the experiences of others.

Third, relationship with Jesus evokes humility. Encounter with an authentic paradox is not merely a conundrum . . . it is *an extra-ordinary experience.* Christians experience Jesus as both divine and human, and it is this that evokes, not simply obedience or interest, but profound awe. There is a depth to Jesus that is unique. One does not take direction from Jesus, but one walks with Jesus into the unknown. One does not learn from Jesus, but one grows in Jesus in unexpected ways. Such humility shuns self-righteousness and confrontation, and welcomes criticism and conversation.

Fourth, relationship with Jesus evokes compassion. The central irrationality of Christian faith releases extraordinary energy for forgiveness, acceptance, and love. Personal transformation occurs not through one's own effort or understanding, but through the intervention of a "higher power" that is beyond understanding. No pride or egocentricity bars the way for empathy and compassion. The motivation that brings people together to talk about religion is not curiosity or competition, but the universality of addiction and victimization. Relationship with Jesus awakens people to the mutual quest for hope.

The forest itself is transparent to the mystery of life. All cultural forms can convey something of the Holy that pervades the forest. It is this paradox that led Paul Tillich to celebrate the richness of cultural diversity and theological perspective—but to warn that all such human expressions are but signs of the divine that are simultaneously employed and shattered by the authentic experience of Christ.

The flowering of incarnational theology in the Council of Chalcedon unfolded in the midst of controversy. The controversy was over the connection between eternal truth and that expression of human experience most clearly associated with "culture": the visual arts. Could the fullness of God be expressed in a picture? What if your picture of the fullness of God differed from my picture of the fullness of God? And was it blasphemy even to attempt to draw such a picture? The noted historian Jaroslav Pelikan describes the answer of Chalcedon to these fears of intolerance:

> All of this—the inspiration [of Christian art] and the challenge [to Christian art] and the justification [of Christian art]—was eventually provided by the person of Jesus, who came to be seen as both the ground of continuity in art and the source of innovation for art, and thus, in a sense that Augustine could not have intended, as a "beauty ever ancient, ever new."[1]

The answer of Chalcedon is repeated by Spiritual Redwoods today. The joy of one's experience with Jesus inevitably inspires description . . . and the pictures that emerge, no matter how beautiful or instructive, will all inevitably fail to satisfy.

Spiritual Redwoods of our pre-Christian era can avoid religious bigotry, and build positive interfaith conversation, by relying on the central paradox of Jesus. As long as the absolute centrality of Jesus for the church *is a paradox*, opportunity for dialogue and mutual respect abounds. Only when the centrality of Jesus for the church ceases to be a paradox, becoming instead a complex, but ultimately understandable certainty, will the specter of religious bigotry become harsh reality.

The tragedy of Christendom was that the mysterious paradox of Jesus affirmed in Chalcedon, could be so quickly forgotten on subsequent battlefields of dogmatic disagreement. Religion that is founded on dogmatic certainties and reasonable propositions works only when culture is broadly homogeneous. When the forest breaks in upon civilization, and culture becomes a tapestry of race, lifestyle, and perspective, consensus over creeds and catechisms becomes impossible—and undesirable! The last legacy of Christendom is inquisition.

> In preparation for a local congregational consultation, Tom sent in advance a videotape describing the systemic reasons Spiritual Redwoods thrive. A few weeks later he checked with the pastor regarding preparations for the event. "We shared the videotape with the Board and some people were alarmed," he said. "So we haven't decided whether or not to allow the congregation to see it."

---

1. Jaroslav Pelikan, *Jesus Through the Centuries: His Place in the History of Culture* (New Haven, Conn.: Yale University Press, 1985), p. 94.

These vain attempts to police the spiritual lives and theological reflections of others represent the last gasp of Christendom. The global village is not homogeneous. Information is readily available to all, and the exchange of ideas and perspectives is already vigorously happening in all corners of the forest. More than this, the Holy is erupting amid the forest in new and unexpected ways. Spiritual Redwoods do not try to control it. They recognize that the core of their own faith is ultimately mysterious, and they seek dialogue with it.

Spiritual Redwoods seeking to represent Jesus in the pre-Christian era must ask themselves a different question from that of the institutional churches of Christendom. They must not ask: *How can this church educate the public about Christ?* This suggests that the church possesses an understandable truth, to which others can and should be persuaded to give assent, the sincerity of which will be demonstrated by conformity to specific behavioral expectations. Such a mission invites religious bigotry. Instead, Spiritual Redwoods ask: *How can this church live in relationship with Jesus?* This celebrates the fact that the church acknowledges a central mystery, which others can and may already experience, the sign of which is renewed hope and personal transformation.

Spiritual Redwoods thus find themselves in constant conversation with culture. They are always sharing—and they are always listening and learning. They are always seeking new ways to participate with

the apocalyptic Jesus,
the healing Jesus,
the addiction-free Jesus,
the equipping Jesus,
the advocate Jesus, and
the "Heir to Eden,"

who is already working in surprising ways, with extraordinarily diverse people, and gaining unexpected results. They focus all their energies to respond to the spiritual yearnings of the public:

to be changed, rather than to belong;
to be whole, rather than to be safe;
to be free, rather than to be rooted;

to be mentored, rather than to be lectured;
to be vindicated, rather than to be corrected;
to be destined, rather than to be saved.

In so doing, the centrality of Jesus for the church is ever more vital, and the possibilities for interfaith conversations are greatest.

What is it about your experience with Jesus that the forest cannot live without? Inevitably your answer will be a picture, an image, or a story, that will both convey and fail to fully convey, the fullness of that experience.

In the classic American story *The Red Badge of Courage* by Stephen Crane, the young soldier Henry flees from the battle known as "The Wilderness." He is a coward and a snob. He is simultaneously overwhelmed by his own inadequacy, and obsessed by self-righteous pretensions. He wanders through the dangerous forest looking in vain for safety and peace. Eventually he is wounded by a blow to his head, wandering aimlessly on in the woods.

It is then that Henry meets "the tattered man." This man binds his wounds and guides him home. Brambles seem to part in front of "the tattered man," and obstacles vanish before him. His words are consoling and kind. When finally Henry is led safely back to camp, he realizes too late that he never once looked up into the tattered man's face. He does not know what his rescuer looks like, where he came from, or where he went. He does not even know his name.

Henry, wounded and lost in the wilderness, is like many in the tangled forest of the twenty-first century. Civilization has suddenly vanished, and they are surrounded by hidden dangers. When they find their way to the safety and peace of the Spiritual Redwood, they usually recollect some tattered companion who walked with them on their way. This is Jesus. And like Henry's experience with "the tattered man," it is ultimately unimportant what he looks like. All that matters is what he has done.

VISTA FOUR

The Fluid That Flows

Spiritual Redwoods at Worship

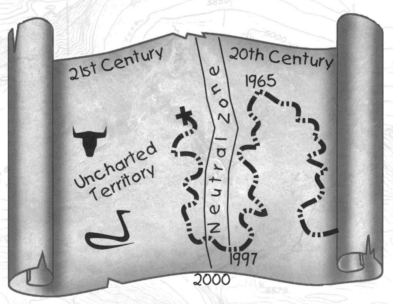

Implementing
indigenous worship
jump-starts transformation.

T here is a fluid that flows through the giant redwood. This fluid flows through the thickest portions of the trunk, the tangle of extended branches, and the network of hidden roots. It flows through the smallest twig and leaf. It bubbles up through the surface of the bark, and moistens the wood to make the tree flexible in the wind. If any branch is broken, this fluid gathers at the place of fracture. Splice the pieces together again, and the fluid rushes forward to renew the withered leaves.

This fluid is omnipresent in the redwood. It is the vehicle that transmits all the nutrition that has been gathered from sunlight and soil. Without it, the smallest bud cannot grow, and the largest branch cannot survive. It is the elixir of life. It is the sap of the tree.

Tree sap is extraordinarily sticky. Not only does the sap flow through the tree, but it seems to be the very glue that holds it together. If it ever stops flowing, leaves fall and branches break. The whole tree fragments into pieces. The sap holds all the diversity that is the giant redwood together as a single organism.

The worship of God is to spiritual redwoods what sap is to the largest of trees. It is omnipresent. It is essential. It is the living water that refreshes and renews. It is the constant, transforming connection with the Holy that is the energy which brings life to every part of the Body of Christ. It is not a bureaucracy that binds the Christian organism together. It is not even agreement about specific doctrines, ideologies, or practices that binds the Christian organism together. The glue that holds the body together is nothing less than the continuous experience, shared by even the smallest buds and branches of the Body of Christ, of the transforming power of God. This transforming power is both reasonable and mysterious, rational and irrational, profoundly personal and equally shared. Worship is the central event in the life of the Spiritual Redwood.

> The worship of God is to spiritual redwoods what sap is to the largest of trees.

When Christendom was alive and well, the cultural forest was held at arm's length. There was little to compete with the traditional liturgies and practices of Christian worship. Worship could be basically the same from church to church, region to region, nation to nation. There would be denominational variety, but within every denomination there would be remarkable uniformity. Experience any worship service, at any place or time, and it would be readily recognizable. The same lectionary texts would be read, the same order of service would be followed, the same hymns would be sung, the same words and movements would be shared, the same music and musical instruments would be used.

In the worship of Christendom, what mattered was simply that you were there. Just being there communicated your faith in God, your commitment to membership in the church, and your comfort with the status quo of Christendom.

Bill was consulting with a local congregation in which worship attendance had gone up and down for years. He asked to talk to a longtime member of the church. "You need to talk to Ed!" he was told. "Ed has a fifty-year pin!" Ed had not missed attending worship at that church for fifty years!

During the interview, Ed disclosed that he was eighty-four years old. He had been raised in a Christian home in which going to church was a regular family affair. He quit attending worship at eighteen to work on a farm a mile down the road. His first child came along when he was thirty-four. He started attending church again, and he had never missed a Sunday since that time.

Bill showed Ed a graph charting worship attendance for the last twenty years, and asked him if he could explain the up-and-down pattern of attendance. His reply stunned Bill. "You're asking the wrong person," Ed replied. "I haven't heard a sermon in more than twenty years!" "What do you mean?" Bill responded. "I was told you had a fifty-year attendance pin." With a sheepish grin, Ed explained that he had a habit of going to sleep. "And if I get to snoring too loud, my wife punches me, and I go out and have coffee with the trustees. They don't go to worship either."

"Why do you even go to church?" Bill asked. "You could sleep as well at home." Ed looked at Bill as if he had lost his mind. "Son," Ed said, "it is my duty to go to church. I must set an example for my children."

Of course, Ed's children didn't live with him anymore. They didn't even live in the same state anymore. The truth is, they didn't even live in the same *universe* anymore!

Ed and his generation faithfully attended church out of a sense of duty to something or someone from their past, whether or not they got anything out of it. Just *being there* fulfilled their obligation to their parents, spouse, children, and ancestors. Ed grew up in Christendom. He lived all his life within a few miles of family. He went to a school without security guards, and traveled on school buses without security cameras. He had never heard of drugs, AIDS, gangs, or drive-by shootings. Everybody shared the same basic values and the same basic beliefs. His life was meaningful because he belonged to a cultural continuity of Christian experience, the primary articulation of which was the institutional church. Ed's life was not a wreck, his relationships were not broken, his future was not ambiguous, his mind did not strain for answers, and his heart did not yearn for healing. He came to church for fifty years simply because it was "the right thing to do."

Today's young adults do not live in Ed's uncomplicated Christendom, where everybody went to church. Their world is far from safe. They live in a world of relentless sociological, emotional, economic, intellectual, and psychological change. If they come to worship at all, they bring questions and expectations that their parents never experienced. They carry burdens of anxiety, ambiguity, and addiction that their parents never knew. If they come to worship at all, the last thing they want is an opportunity to sleep!

In the worship of Christendom, what mattered was correct information. People reaffirmed the doctrinally pure or politically correct truths authorized by the denomination. They gave their assent (either by unison reading or by falling asleep!) to what were supposed to be the universally accepted principles that guided personal reflection and public behavior. The Word of God was always the rehearsed word, the practiced word, or the prepared word, that would correct public error.

Tom was consulting with a congregation in which worship attendance had been steadily declining, and the average age of worship participants had been steadily increasing, for years. This formerly prestigious downtown church had a great pipe organ, a "concert quality" choir, an order of worship so thick it had to be stapled together, pews to hold nine hundred people—and an average attendance of seventy-five. He asked to talk to the most veteran worship leader. "You need to talk to the organist," he was told. "George has outlived three preachers already!"

During coffee hour, Tom asked the organist if he had learned anything in the previous worship service. His reaction was unexpected. "How dare you!" George exclaimed. "The whole point of worship is not that *I* should learn anything, but that *they* should learn something! If only people would worship God properly, the world would be a much better place!" Fortunately, a few lay leaders at the coffee urn restrained George's evident desire to punch Tom in the nose.

Further conversations revealed that, while worship participants prayed fervently for the world to be changed, the last thing they expected was that they themselves might be changed. When worship ended Sunday morning, they didn't want to prepare for spiritual growth disciplines through the week; they wanted to go home to lunch.

As long as the point of worship was to just "be there," one only needed to be an observer of worship to find it meaningful. The great truths of faith could be presented—or paraded—before the mind, and the observing Christians would genuflect, shout "Amen," or simply nod their heads in assent. "Ah yes," the worshiper would say to himself or herself, "these are the truths with which I agree, and these are the people who share my point of view, and this is the tradition that links me to my ancestors." Nothing more mattered. As long as worship was properly done and correctly articulated, all people needed to do was agree, and the world would automatically be a better place.

And yet Christendom is dead. The cultural forest is encroaching on all sides. More entertainments, more diversions, more vehicles of learning, and more opportunities for self-discovery and individual expression compete with Christian worship than ever before. More than ever before, pain, brokenness, emptiness, perplexity, and victimization motivate spiritual yearning. Young and old now live in a different world. The enemy is no longer ignorance, but addiction and idolatry. The solution is no longer better education, but grace. The vehicle is no longer a certified and knowledgeable preacher trained in denominational polity and historical theology, but a safari guide who can coach you through the tangled forest.

"Just being there" doesn't matter anymore; "getting ready for the unexpected" is what is on everyone's mind. Trite phrases and well-worn truisms don't help people through a difficult week. They need a real reason to hope, some practical coaching in faith, and a confidence in ultimate love, just to live one day at a time.

Spiritual Redwoods cannot be grown from the traditional, informational worship of Christendom. The organisms of Christ that once flourished under such worship now wither and die, because the cultural environment has radically changed. Spiritual Redwoods grow when worship

- aims at the heart, rather than at the mind;
- builds harmony, rather than mere assent;
- communicates joy, rather than mere contentment;
- celebrates lifetime covenants, rather than financial commitments;
- sends people into spirituality disciplines, not committees;
- leads people toward freedom, rather than denominational inquisition.

Uniformity from place to place, time to time, congregation to congregation, and worship service to worship service is neither possible, nor desirable, for growing Spiritual Redwoods. The spiritual needs of people, and the cultural challenges of the forest, are just too diverse.

The Purpose of Worship

Worship is a time to give thanks for the transformations that have happened—and continue to happen—through one's relationship with Jesus. Worship is only one part of a disciplined process of Christian living. It must be linked through the week with personal spiritual disciplines, small-group intimacy, and missional activity. True Christian growth does not happen through worship alone, and the Spiritual Redwood does not try to force all aspects of Christian growth into a single hour. Transformation is cele-

> Worship is giving thanks, not being educated.

brated in worship and continues to happen during worship, but it is all part of a larger flow of Christian experience every day and every week. Worship is a time to give thanks for transformations that have happened in your life, even as you have learned to give away to others the fullness that God has given you.

Worship is only one part of a process of Christian living, *but it is a crucial part!* It is the gateway into personal growth and transformation through the week, and as such it becomes part of the transformation process. Worship is the starting point, in which we say to God:

> *"Thank you for being God! If you never do another thing for me, you have done enough! I thank you with all my being!"*

When a person begins here, transformation and growth begin. The worship itself becomes part of the transformation process. People may emerge from worship with new hope and awareness. They may speak of the touch of God that brings healing, help, or renewed meaning. Most of all, however, they emerge motivated to pursue the transformation that has only just begun and the Christian growth that will never end. This growth will only blossom through other parts of the process of Christian living. The Spiritual Redwood is all about growth. Worship is the crucial moment that starts and motivates the process, when renewed and renewing Christians say, *"Thank you for all that you have done."*

Two guiding principles are emerging for the design of worship in the pre-Christian era. First, *worship must be indigenous.* The gospel must be communicated in the language, cultural forms, and technology of the people you are trying to reach. One cannot simply transplant a flower that grows in the south, and expect it to flourish in the north. One cannot impose Western European styles of worship on cultural migrations from around the globe, or classical concert music on generations who have grown up with MTV and MUCH MUSIC, and expect to grow Spiritual Redwoods. To paraphrase Paul's justification for the mission to the

Guiding
Principles

• Indigenous
• Multiple
  Options

Gentiles, visionary Christian leaders are now designing worship to "become all things to all people," that by all means, as many uniquely different people as possible can experience the transforming power of the gospel (1 Cor. 9:22).

Missionaries have always known what it means to be indigenous. Now that North America has become one of the greatest mission fields in the world, Spiritual Redwoods customize worship experiences like missionaries in a foreign land.

Worship designers use the everyday language of the people. No "second" languages, no code words, no ecclesiastical jargon, no vague references to the history of another culture, and no secret rites understood only by the clergy are allowed. Keep it simple, straight and direct, and universally understandable. *(Hint: Convene focus groups with the pre-Christian people in your area to learn their language.)*

Worship designers use the cultural forms of the people. No single musical taste, dress code, behavioral standard, lifestyle, or sense of propriety is elevated above any other. Use the music to which people really listen, dress the way they dress, dance the way they dance, accept who they are, and do purposely what they already do naturally. *(Hint: Find out which radio station charges the most for advertising, and you will find the music indigenous to that area.)*

Worship designers use the technology of the people. Dated resources, limited power supplies, single-source medias, broken equipment, cast-off electronics, and any tool that cannot be easily networked with a computer are all rejected. Technology that is dated, limited, single, broken, cast-off, or incompatible proclaims a religion that is dated, limited, single, broken, cast-off, and incompatible. Constantly upgrade excellence. *(Hint: Take note of the various forms of technology used in conjunction with music.)*

Indigenous worship requires the willingness of worship designers to do anything, change anything, and move anything to better communicate the gospel. Nothing is sacred except the gospel. Nothing is valued more than the transformational impact of the gospel.

Second, *worship must have multiple options.* Indigenous worship leads inevitably to multiple options in worship. There are multiple ethnic groups in every region, multiple demographically and psychographically defined publics in every community, multiple social and personal needs in every neighborhood, multiple tastes and lifestyles in every household, and multiple spiritual yearnings in every individual. One size will not fit all. The gospel must be aimed specifically at the needs and yearnings of a specific people and communicated in the ways most easily accessible to those people.

The cultural units of continuity are becoming ever smaller in the twenty-first century. The missionaries of former centuries could assume a clearly defined national identity. A region would have broadly shared traditions and social understandings. A community would embrace a single ethnic group, and an extended family would share common behavioral expectations. Today, mass migrations, the immediate dissemination of information, and the exploding individualism of people blur national identities, disrupt regional continuities, and fragment neighborhoods. One style of worship service, with a single, constant missional purpose, simply cannot address the needs of people. There is no longer a single "public" to which the gospel must be proclaimed; there are innumerable "publics." Spiritual Redwoods customize worship experiences like entrepreneurs in a free market.

Worship designers target peoples . . . not principles. Their goal is not to gather all people within a practical expression of systematic theology, but to convey specific facets of a larger mystery to specific human needs. They are wholly pragmatic. Worship does not need to be proper. It needs to work. *(Hint: Decide which segments of the population your congregation wants to reach and is capable of reaching.)*

Worship designers target attitudes . . . not ages. They do not rely on broad generalizations about "the youth" or "the elderly," which theoretically remain consistent. They constantly change worship experiences to follow the evolving and shifting attitudes and emotional needs of individuals and publics. *(Hint: Find out the top ten most popular new cars in your area and study the psychographic profiles used by, and readily available from, the dealership's sales department.)*

Worship designers target yearnings . . . not learnings. Their primary purpose is not to educate people in generic truths that should fit every context, but to create an opportunity for a specific human longing to be fully satisfied in an encounter with the transforming power of God. *(Hint: Always have trained people ready to pray or converse with anyone who is moved that day by their worship of God.)*

Multiple option worship requires the willingness of worship designers to listen to people, research trends, and understand in detail the behavior patterns of the community. Their energy is devoted to hearing without prejudice the many voices of the public, rather than reading and re-creating liturgical resources or rehearsing traditional music. Nothing is assumed except the call to ministry (not "The Ministry"). Nothing is valued more than abundant life for each unique human being.

Spiritual Redwoods do not gather the "family" of God, but rather the "peoples" of God. The Body of Christ is made up of many, many parts. The pre-Christian world of the twenty-first century no longer prescribes aspirin and rest for every ache or pain. Today there are innumerable varieties of customized pain relievers to address an enormous and growing variety of human distress.

Transformational Method

Worship in North America is undergoing revolutionary change. Civilized religion has been replaced by the noise of the jungle. The printed page has been replaced by a computer chip. The spoken word has been replaced by interactive drama. Classical music has been replaced by the sounds of nature and the beat of a not-so-distant drummer. The admired preacher has been replaced by the credible faith chorus. The nice, reverent, orderly, down-home, intergenerational, and carefully contained *presentation* of the Holy has been replaced by an unsettling, irreverent, unpredictable, out-of-this-world, cross-cultural, and barely contained *experience* of the Holy. A picture was once worth a thousand words. Now holographic, interactive, multimedia, virtual reality will be worth a billion words. In fact, for worship in the twenty-first century, if you can say it all with words, you've missed the point!

Worship form or style is no longer

Twenty-first-century worship will be extreme but varied.

specific to certain generations. At one time, it seemed safe to assume everyone born before 1946 would automatically value organs, printed liturgies, stately movement, and solemnity. And it seemed safe to assume everyone born between 1946 and 1965 would appreciate synthesizers, guitars, praise choruses, spontaneity, and constant activity. Then a whole new "generation of seekers" emerged after 1965 for whom the only safe assumptions were that worship style would be "extreme" and "extremely diverse." It is becoming increasingly clear, however, that differentiating worship form and style *by generation* no longer fits our cultural experience. A new generation emerges every three years—not every thirty years. The eighteen-year-old who once could inform "the Worship Committee" about the preferences of a fourteen-year-old, now shrugs his or her shoulders in dismay. How on earth should he or she know what a fourteen-year-old would like? That's four years difference in experience! It's a whole different world!

Among the many options of form and style, the one thing that is clear is that the form and style of Christendom worship is no longer effective. Seekers with no institutional church background, and marginal members who are increasingly alienated by institutional church forms, will not participate. Even veteran church members, who are otherwise quite devoted to the institution, attend such worship less frequently, and freely miss worship for two or three months at a time. Since worship is a matter of just "being there" to affirm membership, they just drop off their offering envelopes the next day or send post-dated checks to the treasurer. Since worship is a matter of correct information and assent, they just read the church newsletter and never miss a congregational meeting.

The form and style that is dying on the brink of the twenty-first century emphasizes the printed page, the spoken word, and the massed choir. It is filled with ceremony, historical and institutional jargon, and mysterious symbols. People primarily sit, observe, listen to professionals, and read words written by an unknown authority. Such services include:

- assigned seating and managed movement
- stately music and frequent quiet interludes
- lengthy printed bulletins
- standardized orders of worship

- code words, abbreviations, and unexplained symbols
- organ or piano, robed choirs, and traditional printed hymns
- concert-style anthems and solos
- repetitive or unison reading aloud
- lengthy, monotonous, or complex verbal presentations
- oral communication monopolized by one or two speakers
- ceremony with money.

These services are designed to emulate the unity of Christendom through uniformity in worship. People perform the same acts together, read the same printed words together, sing hymns created by their ancestors together, appreciate the same music together, and uniformly accept the same spoken words as authoritative. Worship creates the appearance of unity among congregational members, denominational franchises, and generations.

Worship designers in the Spiritual Redwood will be constantly monitoring the changing tastes and cultural forms of the various publics of the community. Gone are the days when an ordered framework of "good worship" could be imposed on all fifty-two Sundays of the year, and off-the-shelf liturgical resources could simply be plugged in. The creativity of worship designers handcrafting each worship experience will be pushed to the limit. Whatever the style or form of worship that seems most appropriate for a specific public, all worship in the pre-Christian world will be

Visual! Printed reading material will be cut back or entirely eliminated. Words, songs, pictures, images, and symbols will be projected in color throughout the service. Television monitors, LCD projectors, holographic replicators, and other odd equipment will regularly insert moving pictures into worship.

Surround sound! Sound systems will be state-of-the-art, amplified, and surround worship participants. Music and sound effects will form a continuous background to worship.

Technology supported! Computers, video cameras and monitors, sound mixers, electronic keyboards, and synthesizers will be used by trained volunteer technical support teams. Computer stations at tables or seats in the congregation will directly link participants with worship leaders.

Participatory! Constant opportunities will be provided to respond to, or dialogue with, others in worship. Constant freedom will be ensured to react emotively with others in worship. Drama, testimonies, and dance will regularly be included in worship.

Musical! Music will *always* be indigenous and become the chief vehicle for communication and motivation. Instrumentation and song will be contemporary and in multiple styles heard regularly during the week.

Christian worship in a pre-Christian world will not be a spectator sport, a concert hall, or a lecture room. It will involve all the senses, draw people into faith experience, and motivate mission and spiritual discipline through the week.

Methods change rapidly in a changing world. Not only are "generations" emerging faster and faster, but individuals within generations are evolving in any number of directions. Ninety-five-year-old veterans of the church are dropping out of traditional Sunday worship services, in order to step-dance with the country worship celebration on Saturday nights. Some baby boomers are pushing the limits faster than baby busters—and some baby busters are setting their telephone answering machines to the background music of Gregorian chant. Who can predict what methods of worship will become the most effective vehicles to communicate the gospel to any single public at any given time?

We believe that there are discernible trends for the future. For the next twenty years, the worship designers of the Spiritual Redwood will plan worship around the following three basic tracks. One track includes a modified *"Traditional"* service that will continue to feed those people who, by physical age or mental orientation, continue to find some form of Christendom worship meaningful. The *"Praise"* track will be the dominant form of worship especially among baby boomers, aiming at the heart and involving people in celebration. The *"Sensory"* track is already becoming essential to reach the vast majority of people born after 1965. Its power to enable people to fully experience the gospel will eventually overtake the *"Praise"* track as the dominant method of worship.

The purpose of worship, as always, will be to give thanks for the transformation one has experienced—and continues to experience—in relationship with Jesus. Diversity of tastes and learning styles between generations, and changing preferences and learning skills within any individual's own experience, will call forth variations in transformational method. Over the next twenty years, the worship designers of the Spiritual Redwood will start planning from these basic categories.

Traditional worship seeks to satisfy that decreasing number of people with an appreciation of the institutional church. Participants give thanks in formal, historically grounded, rational ways for the transformations they are personally experiencing.

Praise worship seeks to release the emotions and express the joy many people who were formerly estranged from relationship with Jesus now feel. They find spontaneous, creative ways to interpret and celebrate transformations.

Sensory worship seeks to involve all the senses to appreciate and celebrate the grace which transforms life. Communication occurs less in words, and more in the sights and sounds, images and music, that surround the worship experience.

All three tracks will be implemented with the highest standards of quality possible, and with the best support technology available. The traditional track will decline, while the others increase. Eventually, worship leadership from the traditional track will need to be retrained to participate in the worship teams developing the other two tracks.

Traditional	Praise	Sensory
Rational	Emotional	Real
Information	Celebration	Personal transformation
Knowledge	Discernment	Spiritual growth
Adult-Children Sermon	Adult Orientation	Adult Orientation
Quiet	Semi-loud	Extra-loud
Stately	Casual	More casual
Print	Screen	Computer
Liturgy	Less liturgy	Food liturgy
Creeds	Interviews	Testimonies

Organs	Synthesizers	Guitars-variety
Hymns	Choruses	Secular songs
Choirs	Ensembles	Bands
Explanation of mission	Motivation for mission	All about mission
Faith-telling	Faith-sharing	Faith-experiencing
Bible reading	Biblical drama	This is my story
Oratory	Sermon outlines	Strong content
Directors of music	Worship teams	Worship teams
Liturgists	Drama	Drama
Educational	Experiential	Experiential
Contented souls	Yearning persons	Aching hearts
Offering in worship	Personal decision	Life covenant

The *traditional* track is for those who prefer worship that includes robes, hymnals, creeds, quiet time, and Elizabethan-type music. This track heavily relies on a sermon and one anthem to carry the day. This service is often led by pastor, liturgist, and choir. The strategy of these leaders usually includes printed bulletins, verbal and printed announcements, stately forms of liturgy, and obligatory attendance at worship. Many of the musicians are highly trained and focus primarily on traditional or classical music.

Traditional worship enables people who were born before 1946 to hear the gospel, as well as those of any generation who grew up in the traditional church and never left it. However, traditional worship is not indigenous to the twenty-first-century forest, and it will not be fertile soil for growing Spiritual Redwoods. Please do not misunderstand. Traditional worship grew Spiritual Redwoods for many centuries and will continue to nurture many people who grew up in the first half of the twentieth century. The soil has simply lost its nutrients over the years. Therefore, this track of worship is disappearing.[1]

> In the twenty-first century, worship will be a collage of cultures.

---

1. Pentecostals and independents do show some signs of trying to bring more liturgy into their services. This is a trend worth watching. However, as long as classical or traditional music

Praise worship enables people of all ages to hear and experience the gospel. The praise track is for people who enjoy a celebration that contains ample amounts of highly choreographed, plugged-in, fifties and sixties soft-rock praise music. This is a spectator or entertainment style of worship, with little quiet time and no emphasis on guilt. Content is not nearly as important as the style and quality of the music.

Sensory worship enables people born after 1965 to become part of the gospel experience. The sensory track is described as an experience, not an education or celebration. This experience is encouraged by sights and sounds that permeate the room. Video and visuals replace much of the printed or verbal parts of worship. The extra-loud, plugged-in, and turned-up music is supported by visuals. The music is often secular because this generation does not distinguish secular from religious. The primary concern of this group is hope. The visual track takes five to ten hours of preparation for every one hour of preparation for the traditional service. The service is usually led by a team of young, nonprofessionals who are concerned more about communicating the authenticity of their lives and message, than the style of dress, song, or sermon.

As the relationship of computer and television becomes fully integrated and the prices continue to decline, information will be available to the poorest of the poor. Already satellite dishes exist in some of the poorest homes around the world. Kids the world over know Michael Jackson and can sing his songs. This new digital culture is fast-paced, ever-changing, plugged-in and turned-up, and visually oriented. Images and sounds flash through this culture in endless repetition, making the likes of Lawrence Welk, Norman Rockwell, and McGuffy's Reader as prehistoric as the dinosaur. The cultural changes will be more dramatic and sweeping than those of the Industrial Revolution.

What will worship look like thirty to fifty years from now? Only God knows, but once again we believe there are discernible trends.

The further we move into the twenty-first century, the more worship will be a collage of methods. The styles and forms of many ethnic groups, lifestyles, and perspectives will blend in creative ways to shape worship experiences. Since anything is possible, there may even be room for a return of *"traditional"* worship . . . but churches that

---

continues to decline in popularity in the secular world and experiences like MTV continue to proliferate on TV and the Internet, there is no reason to worry about any trend toward a more traditional setting.

wait for it will have died long before its doubtful return! This collage of worship methods will occur faster in Canada than in the United States but will eventually dominate North American experience.

The purpose of worship will continue to be giving thanks for the transformation one has experienced—and continues to experience—through relationship with Jesus. The growing multiplicity of cultures, lifestyles, and perspectives in every community will call forth even greater variations in transformational methods, but worship designers of the Spiritual Redwood will start planning from these basic categories.

Transactive worship seeks to convey the gospel from one person to another. The message "comes across" gaps of skepticism, fear, or curiosity, and guides people to reflect upon, dialogue with, and give thanks for the gospel.

Interactive worship seeks to involve participants in a reciprocal or mutually shared thanksgiving. People grasp opportunities to celebrate, refine, and share the gospel (and their perspectives on the gospel) with one another.

Actualized worship seeks to make faith as realistic and comprehensive as possible. The reality of the individual and the reality of the gospel merge into one. Thanksgiving is "made real" in the mental, emotional, and physical world of the participant.

All three tracks will share elements in common. All tracks will allow children options to be fully included in worship. All tracks will emphasize music, and use indigenous instrumentation linked to ethnic or cultural heritage. All tracks will be informal and casual. All tracks will link worship participants with processes of Christian growth through the week. All tracks will be planned by worship design teams.

Transactive	*Interactive*	*Actualized*
Questioning minds	Aching hearts	Yearning persons
Insight into faith	Interaction about faith	Shared faith experience
Understanding	Discernment	Empathy
Topical presentations	Topical conversations	Personal coaching

Indigenous responses	Dialogue	Verbal and nonverbal expressions
Indigenous affirmations	Personal witness	Contextual mission statements
Guided meditation	Dance and drama	Film and computer simulations
Guided movement	Spontaneity	Concurrent optional activities
Sitting with friends	Sharing with intimates	Growing with cell groups
Contemporary choir	Ensembles	Bands
Songs of faith	Choruses	Music and sound effects
Faith telling	Faith sharing	Faith experiencing
Bible reading	Biblical drama	This is my story
Offering	Personal decision	Life covenant

The *transactive* track is designed for those who have more caution or curiosity about Christian faith, or who like the predictability of a more structured and guided worship experience. This style of worship may be well suited to seekers who want to "look it over" before "jumping in"—and to some remaining traditionalists who rely on authorities to guide their movements and thoughts. Worship forms may include ensembles, indigenous spiritual songs, contextual affirmations of faith, and responsive readings handcrafted by a worship team. Opportunities for guided meditation will be supported by visual images and contemporary music, and they may involve exercises for body movement and stress relief. They will always be accompanied by methods to communicate questions or concerns. Worship will be guided by identifiable leaders. Participants may have greater anonymity in the service, or greater detachment to observe and purposely reflect on, or respond to, the worship. However, participants will leave worship with an air of eagerness and often comment, *"I am glad I came . . . I now realize something I never understood before."*

The *interactive* track is designed for those who prefer to be actively involved in worship, and who find creativity and spontaneity most revelatory of truth. This style of worship may be well suited to those who want to feel the touch of God, or who seek to interact with the Holy in rational and emotional ways, or who yearn to discuss ambiguous issues. Worship will aim at the aching heart, and worship forms may emphasize drama, dance, faith-sharing (followed by opportunities for questions and comments), spontaneous or "handcrafted" prayers, and opportunities for personal commitments. Worship leadership will be shared by several persons in a setting that is highly participatory. The worship team will include counselors prepared to assist participants who are emotionally touched by the worship experience. Participants will leave worship with a sense of joy and often comment, *"I'm glad I came . . . I feel different . . . I feel better!"*

The *actualized* track is designed for those who want to lose themselves in a total worship experience, who are adept at both linear and lateral thinking, and who want to exercise both "right" and "left" sides of the brain. This style of worship may be well suited to those who wish to experience the awesomeness of God, or who seek to empathically sense the faith journeys of others, or who crave personal coaching through difficult times. Worship will involve the whole person (body, mind, heart, and soul) and provide numerous options to customize the experience for personal needs. Music and sound effects will pervade the worship experience and may include secular music and voices from nature. A band emphasizing rhythm will lead worship, and melody will be more important than lyrics. Participants will not only hear about or share faith, but *experience* the life struggles or faith commitments of others. They leave worship deeply sensitized to the life and faith experiences of others and often comment, *"I'm glad I came . . . I am ready for mission!"*

These three tracks of worship method will have endless variations. Whatever the variation, however, worship will be customized and crafted to be appropriate to surrounding subcultures. Worship method will not be like a reusable eating utensil, indifferent to the food that it contains. Instead, method will be like an edible utensil that is itself food to be consumed. The media will be part of the message.

Transformational Focus

Just as worship is undergoing revolutionary changes in form and style in the emerging pre-Christian world, so also it is discovering new missional purposes. The worship of Christendom could assume that worship participants all shared a foundational biblical knowledge, theological awareness, and Christian commitment. This basic knowledge, awareness, and commitment just needed to be refined, deepened, and guided for the correct purposes. The Christian community needed to articulate the common doctrinal agreement or ideological perspective shared by the church, and in so doing correct wayward or deviant perspectives and rebuke growing secularity. Christian worship would be carefully prepared by authoritative leaders and uniformly celebrated throughout Christendom. The Word of God was important, but the worship of Christendom assumed that *the rehearsed Word would correct public error.*

As the cultural forest invades the carefully defined boundaries of former Christendom, Spiritual Redwoods recognize that worship will have wholly different missional purposes. Nothing can be assumed any longer. There is no foundational biblical knowledge, theological awareness, or Christian commitment. People who do not know the Lord's Prayer, and who have no knowledge of a "New Testament" or "Old Testament," do not need a common lectionary to take them into the distant corners of Scripture. The forest contains a riot of spiritual yearnings and superstitious ideas. Pain, struggle, low self-esteem, addiction, personal confusion, and social disorder are the norms of the forest. There is not one homogeneous society in North America, but many fractious publics. There is not one cultural consciousness, but many competing cultures.

The worship focus that is increasingly irrelevant on the brink of the twenty-first century educates people for membership, communicates huge amounts of theological information and institutional data, and presumes to be the only opportunity for adult Christian education in the week. Such services include:

- printed bulletins and institutional announcements
- traditional hymns with abstract theological words
- liturgies designed by unknown people coded to the liturgical calendar
- corporate apologies and assurances
- responsive or unison readings
- historical or denominational creeds
- lectionary readings prescribed by the denomination
- expository preaching designed to provide correct information

- designated children's messages repeating correct information in simpler language
- verbal descriptions of denominational mission
- financial offerings aimed at the church budget.

They are designed to inform people what is correct or pure, celebrate common agreement, identify the lines of difference between institutional "insiders" and "outsiders," and send the "insiders" home to lunch confident that they have given money to pay somebody else to do professional ministry.

As always, the purpose of worship is to give thanks for transformations that one has experienced—and continues to experience—in relationship with Jesus. The worship designers of the Spiritual Redwood will monitor the changing human needs (physical, emotional, mental, and spiritual) among the publics of their community. They will design worship, using appropriate indigenous forms and styles, to have a specific transformational focus. They will start their planning from these basic categories.

Healing! Worship helps people give thanks for their experience of the touch of God that heals, comforts, and makes whole. Addiction is the top health issue of the twenty-first century, as people are trapped by habitually destructive behavior patterns that destroy life.

Coaching! Worship helps people give thanks for their walk with Jesus, their discovery of mentors and guides, and their opportunity to find their way in daily living. Confusion in the midst of moral and spiritual ambiguity is the dominant lifestyle issue, as people are lost in the cultural forest of the new era.

Cherishing! Worship helps people give thanks for that which is truly important and life-giving. Gratuitous evil, meaninglessness, and oppressive triviality are the leading sources of depression and suicide among the creatures of the forest.

> Model worship around the biblical journey, not abstract institutional forms.

Rejoicing! Worship gathers the healed, the lost, and the accepted in a united expression of pure joy. The focus of exultation is the relationship with Jesus that has made hope a reality.

These four basic tracks of transforming foci will include the following elements and emphases. The patterns of worship in the first three tracks are purposely modeled on biblical journeys, rather than abstract or institutional forms. The pattern of the last track gathers the themes of the first three in a united thanksgiving.

The *healing* track (reminiscent of Paul's Damascus road experience) is designed for those who are hurting, aching, addicted, burdened, trapped, or victimized. The Word of God is celebrated, but *it is the unrehearsed Word that will reveal the truth*. People can experience the touch of God that heals, frees, and makes people whole (either in sudden life change or as part of an unfolding process). Compassionate people pray for them, and help them establish contact with God. They begin to understand who this Higher Power is that is responsible for their experience of grace. Their self-esteem is increased, and trusted mentors share their faith. Opportunities to make new or renewed Christian commitments are provided, and people describe themselves in connection with Jesus. Worship motivates them to participate in recovery groups or twelve-step programs through the week. Participants leave with a sense of eagerness, and often comment, *"I'm glad I came . . . now I have further reason to live one more day!"*

The *coaching* track (reminiscent of Luke's Emmaus road account) is designed for those who are confused, lost, bewildered, anxious, afraid, or just plain empty inside. The Word of God is celebrated, but *it is the mentored Word that guides through ambiguity*. People can experience a companionship with Jesus that will guide them through ambiguity, and provide them with practical help for living the next week. They hear, reflect on, and discuss the teachings of Jesus and the stories of biblical people, and discover for themselves ways in which all this influences the lives of people today. They purposely share food together—perhaps in some form of sacramental communion, or simply as a common meal—conscious that the spirit of fellowship is a revelation of the presence of God. They share faith stories and life stories and build trust out of diversity. Participants emerge better prepared to share their story for the benefit of others and often comment, *"I'm glad I came . . . I thought the service spoke just to me!"*

The *cherishing* track (reminiscent of Philip on the Gaza road) is designed for those who are lonely, isolated, and alienated, or who feel small, insignificant, or ignored. The Word of God is celebrat-

Healing (Acts 9)

"Seeing the Light"
Freedom from addiction
Healing for hurts
Affirmation

"Hearing the Voice"
Personal prayer
Compassionate intercession
Basic Bible reading

"Befriending Ananias"
Mentored faith-sharing
Therapeutic ministry
Kindness

"Going Public"
Invitation to commitment
Acknowledgment of Jesus
Courage to risk

"Climbing over the Wall"
Eagerness to spiritually grow
Celebration of life change
Hope

Coaching (Luke 24)

"Burning Hearts"
Companionship
Guidance in ambiguity
Help

"Interpreting the Word"
The life-work of Jesus
Daily life applications
Bible biographies

"Hospitality of Christ"
Breaking bread
Table fellowship
Inclusive support

"Revelation of Christ"
Insight
Recognition of Jesus
New strength

"Return to the City"
Readiness to witness
Readiness to grow
Joy

Cherishing (Acts 8)

"Seated in the Chariot"
Bonding in Christ
Awareness of destiny
Purpose

"Interpreting Promises"
Prophecy and assurance
Advocacy and justice
Eternal truths

"Passing Through Water"
Cleansing
The way of new life
Celebration of the body

"Sharing the Sacrifice"
Appreciating the cross
Following Jesus
Daring faith

"Going One's Way"
Mission purpose
Partnership in mission
Love

Rejoicing (Luke 19)

"Bartimaeus"
Saving faith
Healing power
Merciful kindness

"The Rich Ruler"
True priorities in life
Absolute trust in God
Assurance of salvation

"Zacchaeus"
Finding the lost
Accepting the pariah
Satisfaction for the seeker

ed, but *it is the cherished Word that embraces mystery.* People can bond with Christ and celebrate their particular destiny in the unfolding plan of God. They gain an eternal assurance that their lives are worthwhile, and that their gifts are of value in fulfilling God's purposes of eternal rescue and justice. They feel a sense of cleansing and renewed life—perhaps celebrated in baptism or a remembrance of baptism—conscious that God has personally identified each one as of infinite worth. The sense of unity with Christ, and with one another, is awesome and leaves people speechless. The action of Christ for salvation fills them with generosity, and they emerge from worship in partnership with other Christians for mission. They often comment, *"I'm glad I came . . . I am loved and ready to love!"*

The *rejoicing* track (reminiscent of the Jerusalem road) is designed to unite all those who participate in the Spiritual Redwood and who are motivated by varieties of personal and spiritual needs. The Word of God is celebrated, but *it is the "joyful noise" that celebrates the goodness of God.* Even as the single journey of Jesus along the Jerusalem road includes celebrations of grace for diverse personal needs, so also people who have experienced grace in many ways unite in a celebration of joy. They celebrate *healing* (as in the story of Bartimaeus), *coaching* (as in the story of the rich young ruler), and *cherishing* (as in the story of Zacchaeus). In the end, it is all one road. The full diversity of people touched by the power of God lines the road to spread palm branches and garments before Jesus, and

> the whole multitude of the disciples [praises] God joyfully with a loud voice for all the deeds of power that they [have] seen, saying, "Blessed is the king / who comes in the name of the Lord!" (Luke 19:37-38)

The *rejoicing* track is the destination to which all roads lead. It is the entrance into Jerusalem in the company of Jesus. This worship track communicates the compelling urgency for thanksgiving that asks for nothing more, and that spills over into loving service in the world. It is the final answer of Jesus to the cultural forest surrounding the Spiritual Redwood: *"I tell you, if these were silent, the stones would shout out!"* (Luke 19:40).

Once again, these four tracks of worship will have infinite variations. The worship designers of the Spiritual Redwood will be constantly adjusting the missional purpose of worship to the changing needs of the community. Some people will go to one track of worship, and some to another. Some will change worship patterns to attend a different track, because their spiritual needs have changed over time. Others may attend all four tracks of worship, because each touches their lives in a distinct way. No matter what track of worship they attend, each track helps them build a continuing discipline of faith through the week, and motivates them simultaneously to share faith and do beneficial services for others.

The varieties of worship offered by the Spiritual Redwood have distinctly different forms and missional purposes. They will always be highly visual, surround people with sound, utilize up-to-date technologies, promote participation, and emphasize music over the spoken word. The Spiritual Redwood can anticipate in advance some of the criticisms of Christendom, no matter which of these tracks is attempted.

"Your worship options encourage selfishness! Good worship should be self-sacrificial. It should lead people to deny themselves, surrender personal benefits for the good of the whole church, and give to others until it hurts." Yet the worship designers of the Spiritual Redwood know that the cultural forest is filled with broken people with low self-esteem. They will do nothing out of obligation or guilt. Only when they are healed and affirmed will their generosity overflow to others. They will give, and give generously, not because they love an institution, but because their lives have been connected with God. Spiritual living will not be a painful sacrifice, but a joyous affirmation.

"Your worship options encourage irresponsibility! Good worship should be corporate, not personal. Good worship should motivate people to do good, not just feel good." Yet the worship designers of the Spiritual Redwood know that the cultural forest is inherently ambiguous and filled with the lost and confused. They will treat all authorities with skepticism, and appraise all education for how well it helps them live each week. Only when they build trust in mentors, dialogue with honesty, and discern for themselves what is right, will they take any risky action. They will do good . . . but only if it feels right.

"Your worship options promote ignorance! Good worship should educate people to interpret Scripture correctly, and understand faith accurately,

and behave properly." Yet the worship designers of the Spiritual Redwood know that the problems of the cultural forest go far deeper than mere ignorance. The core problems of the forest are about being trapped, being lost, and being incomplete, the resolution to which can never be achieved with mere information. First people must experience grace, and then they can be coached to understand that grace. The standards of scriptural interpretation, faith, and behavior can no longer be established by an institution demanding obedience; they can only be discerned and owned by the creatures of the forest themselves.

"Your worship options sever continuity with our Christian heritage! Good worship should recite the ancient formulas, remember the heritage of the past, and repeat the practices of our ancestors." Yet the worship designers of the Spiritual Redwood know that the yearning of the forest is not to return to a past that can never be recaptured, but to find new ways into the future. There is nothing sacred about the music or musical instruments, liturgies or creeds, polities or practices of our ancestors. Indeed, Spiritual Redwoods recognize that the only true continuity with our Christian ancestors is that *all that really matters is the gospel.*

The truth is that the Spiritual Redwood no longer believes in "good" worship at all. In the new pre-Christian era of the twenty-first century there is only *appropriate* worship, *helpful* worship, *indigenous* worship. All that is done in worship should be done with the highest quality possible, but the ultimate worth of worship is not that it matches an abstract standard of perfection determined by an institution, but that it truly celebrates and shares abundant life in Christ.

> Good worship is whatever transforms lives.

A Practical Look into the Future

Take an imaginary trip with us to the year 2020. Many traditional Christian churches have disappeared. These were churches often linked to huge denominations: organized as machines, dependent on clergy, preoccupied with institutional membership, and worshiping in uniformly traditional ways. Church buildings stand vacant, or have been converted into apartments or social service agencies or restaurants, or have been torn down and their stained-glass windows sold to antique dealers. Nevertheless, there are thriving Christian churches inviting widespread interest and participation. They are a different kind of church. They are located in rural areas, small cities and towns, and large cities and populous regions.

The Church of the Living Water

You have recently been transferred by your business for a fifth time in three years, and have relocated your family to a small town or small city. You want to go to a good church, not just because your kids need to be surrounded by Christian values, but because you are continually anxious about tomorrow and need to continue a spiritual discipline, and because your husband has prostate cancer and needs personal spiritual support. You use your TV to browse through the virtual pages and find a description of *The Church of the Living Water.*

You quickly see that the church gives you several choices that week. You could go to the "Coaching and Conversation" event on Sunday morning, and stay for lunch and small groups in the afternoon. Or, you could go to the "Praise" celebration on Sunday night. Since you want to deepen the transformations God has been working in your life, and since you learn best through multimedia, you decide to go to the "Growing in Gratitude" experience on Wednesday night.

The church building is modern, utilitarian, and easy to find because it is located at a large intersection. Parking in the "Guest Parking" section close to the front doors, you walk up the illuminated walkway to be greeted at the door. The band is already playing, and music fills the air. It is a mix of New Country and Rhythm and Blues—just what you like to hear on the radio commuting to work. You bring your little girl to a well-equipped Child Care Ministry superior to the best day-care facility in town, pocket the security receipt without which you will not be able to enter the Child Care facility to reclaim your daughter, and head toward the music.

First, you pass through the Food Court. The church operates a franchise of your favorite international coffee shop, so you buy your favorite drink and carry it with you. You're in a hurry, so you only glance at the bright, interactive video displays of all the missions of the church which surround the Food Court. Now you enter the worship room. Chairs have been arranged around small, round tables, and you find a place to sit. On each table is a small keyboard and monitor.

The music leads you through many moods. Sometimes you listen to "secular" songs you hear every day, and sometimes to music with a specific Christian message. People may applaud the band, and certainly feel free to talk with one another around the table. On the walls around you are projected images and television monitors. Songs may be integrated with film clips and pictures from everyday life around the world. Other projection screens flash the words of the songs, prayer requests, and key verses of Scripture. Using the computer keyboard at your table, you key in a prayer request for your husband's battle with cancer. Around the room, some people may stand or kneel in prayer, while others open their Bibles to identify key verses. Musicians begin to share songs with brief comments about purpose and meaning. They invite you to sing. Soon people are singing songs with enthusiasm, relying on memory or words projected on screens.

As worship unfolds, it is clear that a worship design team has a complex flow running smoothly. You join in prayers offered by a variety of people; watch a drama depicting real, faithful people struggling with a difficult moral issue; and see and hear stories from the missions church participants are doing in the world. On more than one occasion, you use the keyboard and monitor to gain access to the Bible and Mission data banks of the church to answer a question or pursue an idea.

Eventually, the music is softened and lights dim, so that a member of the worship team can share her story. "This is my story," she says. "This is a challenge I faced, and the way God helped me to overcome it." Some people ask questions following the story. Some are moved to tears and also to laughter. As the music returns and gets loud, it carries a ring of confidence and hope. Visuals around the room communicate opportunities for further study, conversation, or mission activity.

As you leave, you pass through the book room to browse. You buy the video of a story shared in a previous worship service that is of particular interest to you. You pick up your daughter, who excitedly tells you about her experience with the interactive Christian computer programs in the Child Care Ministry. Eventually, your whole family finds options within the worship life of the church. Your husband regularly attends the "Coaching and Conversation" event on Sundays, and participates in a small group of people fighting cancer. Your family together often attends the "Praise" celebration, in which parts of the service are aimed specifically at children. You continue to involve yourself in the "Growing in Gratitude" experience. After all, you have a lot for which to be grateful!

The People of Hope

You live in a rural, agricultural community and work on a farm. People are not particularly wealthy, and community services and centers are few and far between. You had a serious problem with alcohol, but a twelve-step program has helped you overcome it—for today. A mysterious Higher Power has helped you, but you would like to go deeper into this connection with the divine. You decide to go to church. You could look in the phone book. Better yet, you could use the kiosk in a community store to gain access to the virtual pages (something you learned to do in fifth grade!). However, you decide just to ask people, "Where's a good church?" And they say, "There! There's a good church!" And you come to *The People of Hope* community church.

The People of Hope offers you choices. Several Christian congregations have banded together around a common vision, in various locations and at various times, and their worship teams share resources and talents. You could go to the "Eternal Truth" service on Sunday nights, with New Age and Light Rock music, in-depth discussion of faith and values, and detailed Bible study—but that seems a bit beyond your current abilities. Or you could go to a "Mentoring" service on Wednesday nights in another location, with mixed modern music, strong faith-sharing and conversation, and interactive experiences—but at the moment you feel rather shy. You could even go to a "Traditional" service in a different location, with a fine sanctuary with pulpit and pews, traditional hymns, and an advertised preacher known for great oratory—but you find that too boring. Finally you decide to go to the "Healing" celebration on Friday nights, because it conveniently follows your AA group breakfast on Friday mornings.

When you arrive at the little country church that is the location for this service, parking along the highway is jammed. The country music from a local band (one of the spirituality cell groups of *The People of Hope*) fills the air. A coffee urn in the vestibule allows you to grab a cup, people greet you cheerily using first names only, and you feel right at home.

In the worship hall you notice a few things. First, all the churchy hardwood has been eliminated. There is no chancel furniture, only a stage. There are no pews, only movable chairs. Second, there is no printed material to juggle. Everything is projected on a screen. On a wide-screen television there are film clips playing or images displayed. Third, there is no podium or cross. There are microphones all around the room, and a huge, handmade dove suspended from the ceiling. Finally, you realize that they must have completely rewired the old building to boost electrical capabilities for all the amplifiers, video, and sound equipment.

The music is loud and rhythmic, and your toes are tapping. Projected images display many contrasting "before" and "after" pictures from the personal experiences of modern people. Worship leaders assure participants of their welcome. Prayers for others are offered, with some participants adding their prayers aloud using a convenient microphone, and others sending forward a piece of paper with a name or concern that is read aloud. Together they say the Serenity Prayer, the words for which are also projected on the screen. The band backs up a soloist. You can see people singing to themselves the songs of the band.

Eventually, one of the worship team shares his story of struggle and victory. You feel as if he is talking specifically to you. Others respond by offering advice and encouragement which adds to the story. Bible stories help clarify who this Higher Power is that so powerfully rescues the lost. Tonight, the Bible story of Paul on the road to Damascus is presented on a ten-minute videotape that was prepared through the week by another spirituality cell group of *The People of Hope* a month before.

You are invited to join others in a public commitment to continue your discipline of abstinence, and to walk one day at a time with Jesus. Projected visuals communicate various cell groups and mission teams that you can join. Some will help you in your continuing struggle, and others will help you reach out effectively to others in similar need.

After the service, you talk with new friends, pick up some free literature on addiction recovery and Bible reading, and sign up for a small group conversation next Monday with a trained volunteer leader you have just befriended. You leave feeling good. You feel encouraged. The healing continues to work its way into your soul and transform your life.

The Virtual Church of the Resurrection

You live in a large city or populous region. Motivated by some personal need, or by some commitment to a spiritual discipline, you want to worship. Since you've never been to church before, you browse the virtual pages. From the list of choices, a Christian spiritual center stands out from the rest—*The Virtual Church of the Resurrection.*

You quickly see that the church gives you several choices that day. You can try the Seekers Introduction Center, or the Interactive Conversation Area, or you can experience Virtual Time. Lately you have been worried about family crises. You decide to try out the Conversation Area. Here's what you might find.

Upon entering the Conversation Area, you see people sitting around tables of four or five, eating whatever happens to be the "in" food of the decade available from the food court in the lobby. You notice that there are two empty chairs at each table—and the people at each table are in deep conversation about something. You soon realize that the topic of the day is flashing on a virtual, wraparound screen that can be seen by everyone in the room no matter which direction they face. The screen is nothing more than an inexpensive holographic projection. The topic of the day is *How to Face Crises with Children.*

You pick out a table and sit down. In the middle of the table you notice a holographic imager. In front of each person is a tiny holographic responder. In a small church, the responder resembles a tiny keyboard or microphone, with which you would punch in or voice-activate your choices. Since you are in a large church with greater resources, the responder is a state-of-the-art thimblelike apparatus. You're already familiar with how this equipment works, since it is equal in quality to what you already have at home or at work. You put the thimble on the tip of your finger and direct mental commands to record your choice of the issues or perspectives most important to you related to the topic *Facing Crises with Children.* You feel right at home.

Soon you are in an earnest discussion with the people at your table. The ideas and issues they are discussing are listed on the screen beneath the topic of the day. Options refer to different people, music, and biblical texts that throw light on the day's topic. The "people" options this day are Abraham and Isaac, or Mary and Jesus, along with one parent-child option currently in the news. The "music" options consist of a variety of current music that connects with the subject. The "Bible" options identify relevant Scriptures. The options your table chooses, and the issues they prioritize, will eventually contribute to the style and missional purpose of that day's worship. *The worshipers will choose the music, the conversation focus, and the holographic people with which they wish to converse.*

As each table makes its choices, the room comes alive with sights and sounds. It is Pentecost! Each person hears his or her choice of music. The wraparound screen displays a constant flood of images based on the individual responses of all the people. Soon the two holographic images chosen by your table, Mary and Jesus, sit down and engage your group in a conversation about what it is like to be a parent and a child facing a crisis together. The holographic images have a database that includes all of the combined knowledge on the topic.

Eventually each table summarizes their conversation, and their comments, questions, and concerns are routed to a quantum-size computer embedded in the brain of the "Faith-Sharer" (preacher) backstage. She quickly formulates the conversation piece based on her personal experiences. She stands in the middle of the room and shares her story, pausing now and then for reactions from the worshipers. The music you have chosen returns again, and you are given even more options to explore this, or related, topics. You may leave whenever you wish. As you leave, you're handed a virtual reality, interactive video of the day's worship so that you can relive and broaden your conversation with Mary and Jesus throughout the week.

Since your experience was so helpful, you decide to return for a second visit. This time you choose the Virtual Time. As you walk into the building, you are directed to a screen with yet another set of options. This morning you can choose from a variety of experiences, ranging from a conversation with Judge Deborah or an experience with Paul called "Shipwrecked."

Since you are a lover of the ocean, you choose "shipwrecked." You're directed to holodrome room number two. As you enter, you virtually move back in time to the first century. You're standing on the shores of the Mediterranean. You can smell the sea, hear the gulls, feel the salt spray. Walking across the sandy beach, you hear a man arguing with the sailors about the trip. The man doesn't want to go, but the crew overrides him and votes to go, so you hurry to board the ship.

On the way to Malta the ship encounters a violent storm. You hear the thunder and see the lightning. You even take a pill for seasickness thoughtfully provided before entering the holodrome room! Suddenly you find yourself shipwrecked! You are in the water; the water is coming up over your head. Suddenly a long wood plank bumps you and you grab on. As the moon rises, you notice a man on the other end. You soon learn his name is Paul. You can see Paul's confidence. You can just catch his muttered prayer. For the next hour you and Paul discuss life and how, if we're not careful, it can drift along going nowhere. "If you get another chance," Paul asks, "what are you going to do with your life?" You talk about your own sense of inadequacy facing crisis. "Jesus is like this plank," Paul replies. "Sometimes he is all you've got left to hold on to. When you reach that point, you're close to faith."

You finally swim ashore. You are a witness to a variety of miracles accomplished by Paul and watch the amazement of the sailors. While you smile at their simple speculations that Paul is divine, you begin to understand why Paul commands so much respect.

The words of Paul fill your head as you leave the holodrome. You almost don't notice a large screen over the exit reminding you that counselors from the church are present in the rooms to the left and right, ready to help you "debrief" your experience of shipwreck. For now, you walk on. Perhaps next time you attend the Virtual Church of the Resurrection you'll be ready to talk about your experience.

Several weeks later, you are sitting with a friend drinking coffee. You are still pondering your experiences with Mary, Jesus, Paul . . . and remembering the story of the faith-sharer. Your friend expresses an interest in this provocative, inspiring, helpful place. He has his own problems!

Since your friend is a rather timid, old-fashioned fellow, this time you choose the Seekers Introduction Center. Entering the multipurpose room, you choose to sit anonymously in the back. A greeter welcomes you and provides you with any material you need to participate, including a brief order of service. Participants are invited to sing a song, the words for which are projected on a screen, and the music for which is generated by a variety of instruments and surround-sound speakers. A worship leader explains the theme of the service. Whenever the leader prays, visual images and symbols are displayed on the screens around the room. Whenever the Bible is read, the words are projected as well. During moments of meditation, a miniature computer in front of you offers options to explore related biblical passages, find the meaning to unfamiliar words, or network a topic to other worship experiences in the church. A speaker shares her faith and invites dialogue. You can remain completely anonymous by keying your question into the computer and having it relayed directly to the earphone of the speaker.

During the final songs, some thought or memory is stirred in your friend. His emotions show on his face. As he rises to leave at the end of the service, a church counselor who has observed the reactions of the participants invites him to talk. Your friend accepts. It suddenly occurs to you, that as long as you're waiting for him, you might avail yourself of the opportunity to talk to someone about your own experiences in the Conversation Area and Virtual Time. An hour later, you meet in the church video store. On your way out, you use your debit card to transfer money to support the church. You suddenly notice all the video displays that describe small groups and ministries supported by the church. "Hmmmm," you say to yourself. "Now that looks interesting . . ."

Sound far-fetched? In February of 1996, Bill shared this scenario for the first time at a conference held at Ginghamsburg United Methodist Church outside Dayton, Ohio. At the end of the session, the pastor of the church hosting the event, Michael Slaughter, told the group that their staff had just talked about the possibility of holographic imagery that very week! The future seems to be closer than we think.

An abbreviated version of the Virtual Church was shared earlier in a periodical. One very prominent Christian authority denounced it as "consumerism." That's sad, because that's the same thing some established, religious folk have said about so many life-altering advances in the methods used by Christians to promote the gospel. And, most often, history has proved them to be less than perceptive.

Clues to Indigenous Worship

The foregoing scenarios give us some clues about the type of worship that will provide an environment in which people can hear the unchanging gospel. Here are a few.

Experience is more important than content. The experience will be created by multiple media. Multimedia and computer-generated visuals are already driving worship in many thriving churches. Pastors won't just write sermons anymore; worship teams will create an experience. The day of the "talking-head" preacher is coming to an end. The goal will not be merely to educate, but to transform lives. The primary way to transform lives will be through interactive sights and sounds.

Worship must be interconnected with everyday life. Artificial distinctions between "sacred" and "secular" will no longer be relevant. Generation X'ers have taught us that dualism of any form does not speak to them. Either everything is worship—or nothing is worship. They do not dress up to come to church, and they do not have to be located in any specifically decorated space in order to worship. Worship space and a healthy environment are equally sacred. Prayer time, work time, and play time are equally sacred. The one flows into the other.

The message must invite participation. People must have opportunity to engage message and messenger in dialogue, conversation, or debate. They must have vehicles for immediate feedback and reflective response. The message must affect people intellectually, emotionally, and motivationally, involving people from start to finish. If a question is asked by a speaker, be prepared for an immediate, shouted answer from the people!

Indigenous music is essential. Music is life itself for young adults. For this reason music and visuals need to compose at least 40 percent of the worship service—and provide background to most of the rest. Music and visuals actually become the liturgy, replacing psalters, creeds, and responsive readings. However, the musical and visual forms must be those which people commonly use every day of the week. The instruments will be those most commonly heard on their radio stations: Good worship music will be defined as any form of music that conveys the gospel to people, whether it be folk, jazz, rap, rhythm and blues, new country, or hard rock.

Music must be felt. Visuals must connect with real life.

The video and sound systems are crucial. The music must not only be heard, it must be felt. Surround sound will be essential. Microphones must be readily available to participants as well as to leaders. It must be possible to project changing images, pictures, symbols, or words quickly, clearly visible to all participants. Money once raised for a pipe organ in the days of Christendom, will now be spent on state-of-the-art sound and video systems.

Technology rehearsals must replace choir practices. Integrating images into the entire service will be one of the most time-consuming parts of indigenous worship. Technology rehearsals will be needed due to the many technical issues involved in integrating the visuals with the songs, announcements, dramas, interviews, conversation pieces, and any other part of the service. Worship teams will include graphic artists and audio technicians. Churches are now gaining permission to use film clips from motion pictures.

High integrity for the leadership is essential. It is imperative that Jesus, and the transformations of person and world associated with Jesus, be central. This means that those who lead worship must have a story to share. Their primary motivation for worship leadership must arise from their experience with Jesus, not merely from musical talent or preaching credentials. Worship leaders share the vision of transformation. They have experienced that of which they sing or speak. They speak, sing, and perform out of their own faith journeys, faith struggles, and faith victories.

Worship teams must replace individual authority. What a gifted individual can do, a talented team can do better. The team must share a profound Christian faith, and members must be talented in their field. The team members must cooperate easily with a common vision, and the beliefs and values they share must be as apparent in their private lives as in their service to the church. The design team will shape the message, the theme, and the supporting elements of the service. The overall worship team will include:

- *the design team* of pastor, music coordinator, and drama coach
- *the leadership team* of faith-sharers, readers, musicians, dancers, or actors
- *the technical support team* for lighting, sound, visuals, and room arrangements
- *the personal support team* of greeters and counselors
- *the prayer team* that is continuously praying for leaders and participants as the worship experience flows.

Constant, uninterrupted flow is crucial. Flow means two things. Everything in the service must interconnect, and there must never be more than five seconds of silence (unless crucial to some dramatic presentation). Any moment that does not contain some activity, movement, experience, or poignant purpose that directly enhances the worship experience will be considered "dead" time. Worship must compete with MTV and Much Music for the souls of the modern public.

(The best way to determine if your worship is on the experiential track is to videotape your worship service and play it on a VCR side-by-side with a television tuned to MTV. The more similarity there is, the more likely it is that your worship is able to share the gospel with people, especially those born after 1965. Next, count the number of times there is complete silence in your worship for more than five seconds. More than one or two such occurrences mean that the service is not indigenous.)

Food courts and accessible refreshments are vital. Food will be a vital part of the worship experience before, during, and after worship. Traffic patterns must allow people to pick up food to bring into the worship experience and allow them to flow easily from the worship experience into a food court or refreshment area. Fellowship over food will be a primary opportunity to discuss worship and connect with opportunities for mission.

Bookstores and resource centers are vital. People will either buy books, tapes, and videos, or take away free material. Lending libraries will be useless and unmanageable. These distribution outlets allow the church to provide additional research, thought, and conversation through the week. Material for handing out or purchase will be displayed topically and be integrated with the themes of the worship experience.

Interactive advertising of mission opportunities is vital. The lobby and refreshment areas will be lined with engaging and informative displays that share all the mission or smallgroup opportunities happening in congregational life. Knowledgeable people will be ready to talk with any inquirer, sign on any new volunteer, or take cash or credit contributions. A cash machine will be available at all times!

Creating Indigenous Worship

Spiritual Redwoods will offer worship options that are extremely different from the traditional worship of Christendom. They will be indigenous, not based on heritage. They will offer multiple options, not uniformity. It is no surprise that some longtime members of our churches who read these pages will find the transition difficult.

> Establishing an indigenous worship service is one of the most important decisions a church can make.

Experience has revealed over and over again that you cannot simply blend radically new worship alternatives with a traditional service. There may be some room for experimentation, but stress levels rise very quickly. As we have said many times, the creative opportunities to blend the other tracks of worship are infinite. However, you will need to leave your traditional worship service alone. Start new worship opportunities.

After a lengthy discussion on contemporary worship, a woman in her seventies approached Bill with this question: "Why can't these young people learn to like my music?" Bill responded: "Why can't you learn to like their music?" She thought for a moment and then made a remarkably insightful reply. "The answer is the same, isn't it?" She will never like theirs; they will never like hers. She had made a paradigm shift.

> **Have three or four Sunday morning services before trying another day of the week.**

Multiple-tracking need not be expensive or complex. It does require a new attitude of openness. The woman in this illustration couldn't surrender her worship option; the church did not want her to do so! She simply needed to allow others to participate in worship options different from her own. No track is better than another; they are only different, appropriate, and effective for the varieties of personal tastes and spiritual needs.

Establishing an indigenous worship service is one of the most important decisions traditional churches can make. Here are some steps for starting this service.

1. The pastor must be among the supporters of the service. This means that the pastor must be prepared to share responsibility for worship, support the combined efforts of a worship design team, and help equip laity for worship leadership.

2. The core leadership of the congregation must increase support of the process. Emphasize the win/win advantages of adding an indigenous worship opportunity: deeper spirituality, increased participation, and greater enthusiasm for congregational life and mission. Remind them that they will not have to attend this service. They will need to give it equal recognition and financial support. Do not talk about changing or blending any of the present worship services. Talk about "adding" a service that people who do not like the service do not have to attend. Remember that the first question people ask in times of change is, What will I have to give up?

3. Identify the indigenous population for whom the service will be developed. This will require research into the demographic and pyschographic nature of the community, and intensive listening for the spiritual needs of the public. You may well discover more than one group for whom a service might be designed, but do not try to be all things to all people. Start with one service for one target population.

4. Gather a new Worship Design Team to begin the service. Involve leaders connected with the indigenous population for whom the service is being designed. Allow them to determine for themselves the training they will need. Do not give the responsibility to an existing worship committee. Look everywhere for motivated leaders, often among those on the present margins of congregational life and beyond the church.

5. **Gather a Music Team to begin the service.** Involve leaders who are knowledgeable and experienced with the music of the indigenous population for whom the service is designed. The team may themselves be a band or an ensemble, or they may be coordinators who can gather appropriate musicians and musical support technology.

6. **Identify the core values for this service.** Involve the pastor, the core congregational leaders, and the worship and music design teams in this process. What is the purpose of starting the new service? What do we want to accomplish among the target population? What are the essential, nonnegotiable values that surround all worship in the congregation?

7. **Identify the core beliefs for this service.** Involve the pastor, core congregational leaders, and worship teams in the process. What is the purpose of starting the new service? What do we want to communicate with the target population? What are the essential, nonnegotiable beliefs that surround all worship in the congregation?

8. **Visit nearby churches that offer contemporary worship to get a feel for what might work in your church.** Visit as many different denominations as you can. However, don't simply copy what the other church is doing. Make it your own, suited to your talents, values, theology, mission purpose, and whom you are targeting.

9. **Determine the time for and frequency of the service.** Choose the time period that is most opportune for the indigenous population you seek to involve in the service. Whatever the time you choose, avoid changing it. Patience and consistency are important.

The fastest-growing time period in North America for worship is between nine o'clock and ten-thirty on Sunday morning; there is also growing evidence for twelve-thirty on Sunday afternoon. When you have multiple services on Sunday mornings, do not fear having worship and Sunday school running at the same hour. Attendance in Sunday school will not be hurt. In fact, overall attendance will increase.

Another frequent alternative is Friday or Saturday evening. Attempt a service at a time other than Sunday only if you already have three services on Sunday morning—and the one on another day is seen as equal in importance to those on Sunday morning. When you have multiple services through the week, do not fear developing distinct congregational identities. Competition is not inevitable, provided you have support from the pastoral and core leadership and have clearly identified essential values and beliefs. In fact, overall participation in church life is increased, enriched by diversity and invigorated by small-group ministries.

Most new worship opportunities will be weekly events, but limitations in your resources or circumstances among the target population may lead you to begin biweekly or even monthly new worship opportunities. Quality is more important than quantity. Worship services will increase in participation and in frequency only as the quality of worship builds enthusiasm in the community.

10. Determine the place for the service. Choose the setting that is most familiar to the indigenous population you seek to involve in the service. People need to "feel at home." Avoid overly formal and cold settings, in favor of casual settings that encourage conversation.

If you locate the service in the church building, make sure that lighting, sound systems, and air quality are excellent. You may need to move furniture to make room for projection screens, equipment, drama, and so forth. Make sure that the electrical supply is adequate for your technology and that the room is accessible. Rely on flexible chairs, not fixed pews.

If you move the service beyond the church building, make sure the location is easy to find and that parking is adequate. Additional outdoor lighting will be important for safety during evening hours. You will need to have permission to decorate the room and move furniture, and the neighbors need to understand that the worship may be noisy.

Drama departments from local schools usually have someone who will be glad to help. Concert promoters are also helpful, but will charge a consulting fee. Whatever place you choose, avoid changing it. Patience and consistency are important.

11. Build a worship support team. This may include hosts and hostesses, parking lot attendants, child-care workers, technology assistants, and stage crews. Train lay pastors and counselors, for stationing throughout the congregation during worship, who can support participants during worship and pray or converse with individuals following the service. In addition, gather a core group of people from your existing service to agree to be at this service for the first six months.

12. Constantly monitor, evaluate, and fine-tune the worship service. The worship teams must review their efforts, seek out critical comments from participants, and place themselves on a constant quest for quality. The pastor and core congregational leaders need to be ready to assist the worship teams in achieving the highest standard of excellence that is possible in the context of that church and community.

13. Constantly support and expand leadership. Build worship teams as spirituality cell groups, not task groups. Multiple services are very hard on musicians and technology support teams. New volunteers should be welcomed and trained. In time, additional part-time staff may be necessary.

14. Devote twelve to eighteen months to the pilot project. After this, you may need to make fundamental changes in time, location, leadership, or design. Remember that most people in the pre-Christian era have a strong distrust of the institutional church. It takes patience, quality worship, advertising, and word-of-mouth enthusiasm to slowly build support for a new worship opportunity.

15. Now pray for yet another mission! Once an additional service is fully integrated into the community and the congregational life, it is tempting to rest on your laurels. Resist the temptation! Risk yet another worship service aimed at yet a different spiritual yearning or demographic group. Or, invest congregational energy in some other form of mission to which you believe God calls.

Footnote for the Small Church

The single most important factor that limits growth in worship has nothing to do with finances, property, or staff. The most important factor is *vision!* It is the readiness to see the real needs of diverse population groups in your midst, and deploy worship opportunities that effectively involve those people. Indigenous worship need not be elaborate or complicated. It does require a new attitude and sense of mission. When the attitude and vision are there, even the smallest churches can find the money, change the property, and equip the lay leadership to do indigenous worship.

For as little as $5,000 a church can do everything the Virtual Church of the Resurrection did except the holographics. All the equipment a small church needs is a large 55-inch to 80-inch television set, an inexpensive computer, one small software program, a MIDI or guitar, an overhead projector and screen—and one enthusiastic teenager! A somewhat larger church can aim to spend just $10,000 and use an LCD projector instead of a television. A very large church can spend considerably more and use an expensive LCD projector that is as brilliant as a motion picture screen ($80,000).[2]

The software for the virtual room is currently in an embryonic stage. However, inexpensive interactive software is already available for use in worship and Sunday school.[3]

> **The only excuse is that a church doesn't want to do indigenous worship.**

The introduction of the MIDI makes it possible for a church to have a full orchestra every Sunday. A variety of companies sell reverse negative slides for churches to use with overheads and slide carousels.[4] Within a few years, the holographic responder (or whatever it will be called) and the virtual screen, will be priced much lower than an electronic organ. The only excuse left today for the smallest congregation not to attempt indigenous worship is that they just do not want to reach emerging generations and subcultures with the gospel.

Nevertheless, be warned. If a church is more interested in protecting its heritage, than in reaching out like Paul in a "mission to the Gentiles," the development of indigenous worship will be the single most stressful step in church transformation. It will be the single greatest block to transforming a church into a Spiritual Redwood. Proceed with caution . . . but proceed!

---

2. For more information about the various types of equipment available, see the monograph *Worship in the 1990s*, by Bill Easum (21st Century Strategies).
3. One example is the CD-ROM version of "The Father and Two Sons" available from the American Bible Society.
4. Brentwood Music, 1-800-333-9000, 316 Southgate Ct., Brentwood, TN 37027. J & J Graphics and Designs, 39888 John Drive, Canton, MI 48187. Phone (313)453-0697, fax (313)-453-0698. Phil Barfoot Music Company, P.O. Box 4629, Chatsworth, CA 91313.

The indigenous, multitracked worship services of the Spiritual Redwood will lead this Christian organism to interact with the cultural forest in surprising ways. Indigenous worship breaks down stereotypes of theological, ideological, and denominational perspective. Congregations find themselves working in relationship with groups and organizations with which they previously had little or no communication. Why?

- because indigenous worship calls for the Spiritual Redwood to listen to the many publics of the forest more sensitively, compassionately, and honestly than ever before, and
- because multitrack worship calls for the Spiritual Redwood to identify, share, and teach more diverse leadership skills than ever before.

For congregations making the transition to Spiritual Redwoods, this can be both an exciting and stressful time. Social activist "liberals" and evangelical "conservatives" within the same congregation come together to plan and celebrate indigenous worship because it links real people, with real problems, into a transforming relationship with Jesus that brings real change. Churches of different denominations begin to cooperate with one another sharing resources and training leaders. "Mainstream" churches and "evangelical" churches that once were pitted against each other in the community find common ground for ministry. Stories abound across North America of churches with a new vision seeking assistance from other churches, and receiving support joyfully and without judgment or reservation.

Perhaps the most unexpected benefit of indigenous worship, however, is the door of communication that has opened between Spiritual Redwoods and the religious pluralism of the forest. Strip away the religious competitiveness, aesthetic snobbery, and unthinking stereotyping that surrounds worship at the end of the Christendom era, and you will find new friendships and shared ideals. You will recall Tom's story from the foregoing vista about the new understanding between the Christian congregation and the Muslim community. Here is another piece of that story:

Coffee conversations with the Imam often mentioned Moussa. When the war known as Desert Storm erupted, the Christian congregations and the Muslim community found a basis to share prayer services together for the first time ever.

Moussa started attending our worship service as we were moving from informational worship aimed at the head, to motivational and healing worship aimed at the heart. Moussa was a Sunni Muslim. He was Iranian by birth, but had fled to Iraq after the revolution. He rose to the rank of Colonel in the Iraqi air force, and in the subsequent war he had flown missions that attacked his own people and bombed his own villages. After the war, he had floated around Europe, somehow landed in Canada, and arrived in our community. Understandably, he had a hard time fitting into either the Sunni or the Shiite Muslim groups in the city. Yet the local Imam cared about him, and during our coffee conversations about personal transformation, he spoke of him.

Moussa was emotionally disturbed and mentally ill. Given his history, who could be surprised? He came to our worship services because he believed we worshiped the same God, and because he sought healing for his soul. During our worship he would walk down the long center aisle in the middle of the service shouting "Salaam! Salaam!" kiss the faith-sharer on both cheeks, and return to his seat. It scared us all to death! Often he would become so emotionally caught up in the worship that he would leave the service temporarily. We learned that we needed to equip someone to find him and talk with him. Many hours were spent in personal prayer and small group conversation. He believed he could feel hope and wholeness in the services.

Eventually the crumbling social safety net in Ontario failed Moussa. Discharged prematurely from a mental health hospital, he committed suicide by hanging himself in the stairwell of his apartment. Despite the stigma of suicide, the Muslim community proceeded to bury him with full honors, and for the first time ever Christians gathered at the graveside with them. The Christian pastor was the first to throw earth into the grave in the absence of the closest next of kin.

Despite the tragedy of Moussa, blessings have emerged. These first hesitant steps toward indigenous worship aimed at thanksgiving for transformation had brought healing to a troubled mind, forged a new and continuing conversation between two distant faiths, and brought Christians and Muslims together in prayer for the first time in this community. We discovered that we could love each other, respect each other, care about each other, and cooperate with each other, even though we knew that we disagreed with each other about many things.

Indigenous worship can be a gateway into unexpected partnerships. It can break down long-standing distrust, in the common bonds of hope. Big as a Spiritual Redwood is in the forest, there is something even bigger: the transforming power of God. Who knows where these new conversations will lead? One day God will lead us poor humans to a truer harmony of which our indigenous worship is only a sign.

VISTA FIVE

Following the Flow

The Organization of the Spiritual Redwood

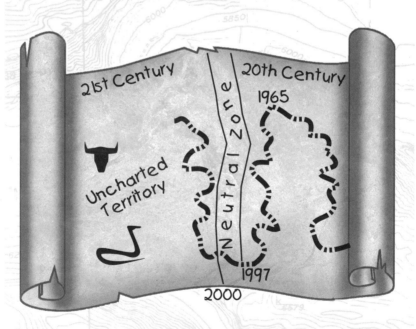

21st Century   20th Century

1965

Neutral Zone

Uncharted Territory

1997

2000

Spiritual
Redwoods live to
organize.

E verything in the forest lives to organize. Each plant, each shrub, each tree adapts itself creatively to its unique and immediate environment. The motivation behind this impulse to organize is more than individual survival. It is more than the survival of the species. The most profound motivation to organize within every organism is simply to flourish. Explorers of the forest are continually amazed by the natural impulse of all organisms to grow, expand, and thrive.

The organizations of the forest are a veritable riot of diversity. The organization that works on the cliff side is not the same as the organization that works in the meadow. The organization of one organism cannot be easily transplanted into the immediate environment of another. Explorers of the forest are continually astonished by the diversity of experimentation simultaneously under way.

The organization that will work in any given environment cannot be easily predicted. No blueprint for construction is available for organic growth. Just as explorers of the forest always find forest paths circuitous, so also the organizational development of every organism is circuitous. There are dead ends and unexpected choices. Promising paths or organizational strategies suddenly lead nowhere, and seemingly unpromising paths or organizational strategies lead to surprising vistas of opportunity.

Although there is neither detailed repetition, nor clear predictability, for the organizational life of the organisms of the forest, there are commonalities which taken together make the difference between organic growth and artificial movement. Organic organizations change constantly, adapt quickly, and thrive over time. Artificial organizations may be easily duplicated, and may be readily predictable, but they change only in dire necessity, adapt slowly, and wear out over time. The forest eventually overwhelms them.

The biggest surprises that await explorers of the forest are often hidden within foliage, behind bushes, or underneath mud slides. These are complex aggregates of rusted metal and tarnished plastic, of infinite shape, size, and variety. They are machines! Sometimes they work (wholly or in part), and sometimes they do not. Press a button, pull a lever, or turn a dial, and the thing starts to click and move. Sometimes the purpose behind the movement of the machine is clear, and sometimes that, too, is shrouded in mystery.

Sometimes these machines are entirely derelict, and sometimes they are still partially preserved, oiled, and maintained by a remnant of gnomes who service the machine even in the midst of the encroaching *forest. The purpose of the machine may be forgotten or irrelevant, but the continued working of the machine has become all important. In addition to the natural camouflage of the encroaching forest, a defensive perimeter has been created to protect the machine. Amid all the sounds of nature, the machine continues to click and whir in the night.*

The most jarring reality about the derelict machines of the forest is not that some of them are still shiny, nor even that some of them are impressive in complexity, but that they are so out of place! The machine in the forest is an intrusion. It does not belong. It is irrelevant. The forest relentlessly attacks and rejects them, like foreign bacteria in a living organism.

Meanwhile, the Spiritual Redwood grows in the forest to immense size and complexity. In common with all organic organizations of the forest . . .

- *the Spiritual Redwood lives to organize*
- *the Spiritual Redwood reveals a riot of diversity*
- *the Spiritual Redwood cannot be easily duplicated, nor can its unique growth be entirely predicted.*

Yet it is the most successful organizational unit of the forest. The multitude of "parts" to the tree grow in endless variety, and yet in a harmony of mutual support. The efforts of the entire tree allow the smallest twig to inch its way toward the sunlight, and the fate of the smallest twig is felt even in the most distant root. Unlike the machine, the organizational unit of the Spiritual Redwood really belongs in the forest. It is attuned to its environment. The health of the forest, and the health of the Redwood, are a single common issue.

The emergence of the Spiritual Redwood in North American culture signals a revolution in church organization. The age of repeatable, predictable church bureaucracy has come to an end. It has been replaced by organic organizations that share the common features of the forest:

> The Spiritual Redwood signals a revolution in church organization.

1. **The emerging organizations are designed to grow.** Their purpose is not to repeat or protect an ecclesiastical heritage that was their original programming. Their purpose is to expand and thrive in any way that will enhance life with Jesus.

2. The emerging organizations grow in a riot of diversity.
Their strategy is not to clone themselves in as many places as possible, within a uniform ethos of denominational practice. Their strategy is to empower whatever works, in order to overcome any obstacle limiting life with Jesus.

3. The emerging organizations grow in constant, creative chaos. Their life is not repeatable from one ecclesiastical franchise to the next, nor is it predictable within any church from one year to the next. Their life is a constant bubbling of innovation and change, which usually appears to be out of control, and often truly is out of control, the energy for which is entirely devoted to enhancing life with Jesus.

These emerging organic organizations may be both a mystery and a threat to Christians who have grown up with church bureaucracy. They do not do what bureaucracies do. They do not protect a heritage, but create a future. They do not nurture comfortable homogeneity, but aggressively welcome diversity. They do not provide stability, but generate constant opportunity.

The churches described in the Acts of the Apostles illustrate the organizational nature of living organisms. They do not illustrate the organizational nature of bureaucracies. In the age of Christendom, interpreters suggested that this was because the apostolic churches were young and inexperienced. They had not yet matured to the efficiency and uniformity of bureaucratic governance. In the return of the pre-Christian era, however, we have discovered that this lack of resemblance between apostolic churches and church bureaucracy has nothing to do with youthful exuberance. Apostolic churches simply flourished like organisms in the forest.

First, they are designed to grow. They are all oriented around a core vision of life to the full with Jesus, and that core vision is the only benchmark for self-evaluation. As we have already noted in the paradigm of the Philippian church, they build teams, nurture spiritual leaders, grow small groups, and release energy to share the gospel that transforms lives. Their primary purpose is not to give thanks, consolidate a heritage, or leverage power in the community. Their primary purpose is to enhance life with Jesus. It is to *share the glory!*

Second, they grow in incredible diversity. The congregations at Philippi, Ephesus, Athens, Rome (and, presumably, in Ethiopia,

Spain, and India) are all different. It is no wonder that scholars have had trouble standardizing titles of church leadership in the New Testament. They were all different! Tasks, roles, offices, and leadership were different from place to place—and rightly so! The beauty of the diversity of the early churches was not that a Christian traveler could visit a new culture and immediately be at home, but that a Christian traveler could visit a new culture and experience a new expression of life with Jesus. *Only Jesus would be the same . . . nothing else!*

Third, they grow in constant, creative chaos. Each congregation developed in different ways, and at any given time no single congregation could predict with any certainty what it would become. Paul's quarrel with the Corinthian church was not that it was disorderly, but only that its disorderliness went beyond the boundaries of the core vision, values, and beliefs of the Christian movement. Chaos was welcome, so long as it creatively enhanced life with Jesus. Visions could erupt and innovations could emerge, sacraments could be shared in any number of ways and music could be sung with any number of tunes, and the fruits of the Spirit could blossom in any direction—so long as life with Jesus was enhanced for *these* people, in *this* environment, at *this* time.

It is significant that the early Christian movement specifically rejects bureaucratic control. Paul and Silas, Peter, Philip, and many others, are free to respond to visions, develop creative partnerships, and initiate indigenous worship and ministry, without accommodation to predetermined reports, permissions, or procedures. There is no hierarchy of control. The attempt to establish such a bureaucracy reported in Acts 15 fails. The Christian movement simply identifies core vision, values, and beliefs that are the perimeters of church life, and celebrates any and all manifestations of Christian experience within it. Such organic organization, synchronized with the cultural forest, is the very essence of the Mission to the Gentiles.

What follows in this chapter is not a blueprint for creating the organization of a Spiritual Redwood. We cannot simply tell you what to do, nor can we tell you exactly how to do it, because the emerging organization is not a machine. That Body of Christ which grows in your immediate environment may not resemble in any detail the Body of Christ which grows in Bill's environment, or in Tom's environment. We can, however, trace the commonalities, which taken together make the difference between machines and Spiritual Redwoods.

Machine or Organism?

Past wisdom in church development helped congregational organizations evolve bureaucratically from "family," to "program," to "corporate" organizational models. They evolved from intimate tribes led by traditionally selected matriarchs and patriarchs . . . into complex institutions governed by multiple committees . . . into even more complex corporate entities with multistaff professionals and careful divisions of labor. Stress accompanied each point of transition, but denominational leaders and church consultants could help congregations make the necessary adjustments. Unfortunately, as North American culture became radically transformed with the demise of Christendom, none of these evolutionary organizational stages worked anymore. The wisdom of church development sought to replace hierarchy by "flattening" structures and dispersing authority and power to more and more people. Stress over issues of accountability grew exponentially, since integrity could not be "dispersed" as easily as authority. At the same time, the wisdom of church development sought to streamline management, not only to save money slated for professional salaries, but to make the organization more rapidly responsive to changing culture. Stress over issues of coordination grew exponentially, since cultural change always outpaced institutional response.

The issue of "control" dominates the agendas of the institutional churches disappearing in the contemporary pre-Christian era. Church organizations are in constant anxiety about their inability to ensure responsible behavior by leaders and participants, and about their inability to match the frantic pace of cultural change. The issue of control is fueled by the desire to preserve and protect the great and glorious heritage of their institutions. This heritage has denominational and local manifestations, with the former treated as the more expendable. Individual initiative that rapidly responds to emerging cultural needs is feared by the organization. It might undermine the polity of the denomination, or the principles of the denominational founders, or the ethos of the denominational corporation. More significant, it might undermine the traditions of our parents and grandparents, or the aura of nostalgia that surrounds local property and religious practice, or the influence of the inner core of local church leaders.

There is a still deeper dimension to this heritage that is being protected. It is the heritage of the organization itself. The transitions between "family," "program," and "corporate" church may have had stresses, *but at least the basic nature of the organization remained the same.* These were evolutionary changes, and part of a single continuum of organizational purpose. The whole point of any church organization, whatever its form, was *to control!* Organizations ensured consensus in opinion, and conformity in behavior. That control might be exercised diplomatically or dictatorially, and it might establish boundaries for experimentation that were narrow or broad, but the whole point of an organization was control. And that is the heritage churches disappearing in our pre-Christian era are trying desperately to protect.

And they all look
JUST THE SAME

Figure 5.1

These church bureaucracies are machines. They may be of endless variety, designed by various denominational polities and theological technicians, but they are all machines no less. They may be simple or complex, showy or shy, liberal or conservative, but their organizations all aim to control. They have a "control center" that directs the activities of the machine. They have a fail-safe mechanism that stops the belts and pulleys if any activity threatens them with self-destruction. They require spare parts in the form of new participants, who can replace those that are worn out. If spare parts cannot be obtained, the machine is programmed to convert the raw material of spiritual seekers into customized institutional cogs for

A machine is a machine, never an organism.

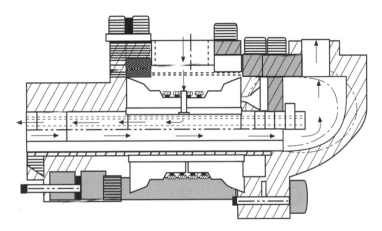

Figure 5.2: The Machine

the mechanism. The machine assimilates data collected from its various divisions or committees, and can even be minimally self-corrective to adapt to changing circumstances. Nevertheless, the machine cranks out an essential line of products that culture may or may not want, but which the designers of the machine believe culture requires. Denominational technicians or religious experts will service the machine over time, adding clever new programs, oiling the wheels with correct information, and occasionally upgrading the power source with an improved model fresh from Seminary.

Figure 5.3: The Organism

Unfortunately, with the demise of Christendom in the pre-Christian era, it does not really matter whether a church organization is described as a triangular hierarchy, or as an inverted triangular democracy. Nor does it matter if church organization is complex with multiple professional leadership, or simplified with streamlined decision making. Spiritual Redwoods have made a quantum leap away from any "triangular" model. They have left behind any linear decision making whatsoever. They are not about "control."

Spiritual Redwoods are not machines. They are not foreign bodies intruding upon culture, for the purpose of manipulating culture. They are organisms. They are made of the same stuff and substance as culture itself, and understand the health of the church and the health of the community to be a single issue. They are designed for growth, continually redesign themselves for growth, and accept nothing less than growth. Why? *Because enhancing the fullness of life with Jesus is all that matters.*

We cannot repeat often enough that the very nature of organic organizations prohibits any detailed description that can simply be replicated in every context with generally predictable results. The Spiritual Redwood is not a machine. On the other hand, we can describe what might be called the essence of the species. The essence of the Spiritual Redwood is the core vision, values, and beliefs that provide a proscriptive environment for individual expression and emerging mission.

The Essence of the Species: Core Vision, Values, Beliefs

Instead of a "prescriptive" mandate that "prescribes" or lists everything an individual can or must do to fulfill an institutional obligation, the church provides gifted individuals with a *"proscriptive"* boundary within which their innovative energies can be released. Such a boundary identifies limits beyond which individuals cannot go, but within which they are free to use their spiritual gifts in any creative way they choose. In Tom's book *Kicking Habits: Welcome Relief for Addicted Churches*, he described the core vision, values, and beliefs of the organization using the metaphor of an electromagnetic field. This energy field both contained and accelerated the flying electrons and atoms of individual and small-group growth and ministry.

Figure 5.4

Readers who have followed Bill's thinking through *Dancing with Dinosaurs* and *Sacred Cows Make Gourmet Burgers* will know that Bill speaks of a triad of "mission, vision, and values." Essential beliefs were included or assumed in all three categories, and Bill specifically emphasized "mission" in the triad in order to underline the dynamic purpose of the Christian organization to "pass life on to others." Here we will clearly articulate core beliefs as an identifiable aspect of the essence of Spiritual Redwoods, but emphasize that "mission" is the dynamic expression of the totality of vision, values, and beliefs. In a sense, "mission" is a kind of "shorthand" for the unity of vision,

The essence of the Spiritual Redwood is to be and make disciples of Jesus.

values, and beliefs that lies at the heart of the Spiritual Redwood. This is why a brief, pointed, articulate statement of mission is fundamental to growing spiritual organisms. It translates "essence" into "action."

Using the metaphor of the Spiritual Redwood, we might describe the essential core of vision, values, and beliefs to be the *aura of life* that surrounds the organism. It may not be clearly seen by the naked eye, and it certainly cannot be fully understood by scientific analysis, but *it is there!* And it is crucial to the life of the organism. It is sensed by people in the community and by the creatures in the forest of human culture.

Perhaps a more biblical metaphor would be to describe the essential vision, values, and beliefs of the organism as *"the aroma of Christ"* (2 Cor. 2:15). Paul uses the metaphor in reference to the powerful incense dispersed in advance of Roman processions that announced the presence of authority long before the first soldiers were in view. Here, we use the metaphor in reference to the powerful scent of coniferous trees that alerts one to their presence long before they are visible to the eye. The core vision, values, and beliefs of the Spiritual Redwood are the signs that mark the species.

Core Vision

The precise vision that lies at the core of a Spiritual Redwood may vary from one organism to another. Nevertheless, the core vision is always there, and it is always the most critical fact of organizational life. The evaluation of any ministry, and the accountability of any leader, are measured in relation to that vision. This vision is the first thing that is revealed to the creatures of the forest, and it is the last thing that lingers in the minds and hearts of the creatures of the forest. However diverse the ministries of the Spiritual Redwood might become, and however diverse congregational participants might be, this vision *IS the Spiritual Redwood!*

The core vision of the Spiritual Redwood is always linked to the nature of ecclesia, namely, that Christians are "called out" of the world to be disciples of Jesus and to make disciples of Jesus. Beyond this, however, the core vision of the Spiritual Redwood is the unique expression of that mission. It is the unique place or purpose of a specific Christian organization in the divine plan to rescue creation and return to Eden. The vision is the answer to the question, *What is it about my experience with Jesus that this community cannot live without?* It clearly grasps that pivotal, heartfelt experience with Jesus

> **The core vision motivates action.**

which has so changed one's direction in life and activity of living, and which has so filled one's life with joy and meaning that unless one shares it with another, that other person's life will be impoverished. The core vision fills one's life with generosity, overflows in magnanimity toward the world, and is always associated with one's connection with Jesus. Who knows what the vision will be?

The vision will be *a song in the heart.* It is a metaphor or symbol, a rhythm or tune, a picture or experience, the mere presentation of which elicits spontaneous joy and excitement. The vision speaks to the heart, rather than to the mind. It is like a song hummed in the back of the mind while walking, the rhythm to which matches the cadence of footsteps, and which is suddenly raised to consciousness with an unexpected jolt. It is never fully contained in words, and one always feels rather breathless and frustrated trying to communicate it to another person. Yet at the same time, the vision is so compelling that one simply must share it with others—even with perfect strangers!

The vision *makes you feel like nobility!* It uplifts the human spirit, and fills the heart with immense purpose and meaning. It fills a person with impatience and with a burning desire to do something immediately. The specific action required may be unclear. The support of others is helpful, but not essential. It is the vision itself which fills an individual with renewed self-esteem and centers an individual toward a single-minded destiny. It invests a small human life with universal significance and infinite worth.

The vision is *true north for the soul.* It is a permanent, intuitive compass direction for a human being. Every person inevitably strays from the path. Life is an endless experiment and course correction. The vision brings one back to the true path. One only needs to pause, refocus, concentrate on the vision, and new clarity for action emerges. The vision is like a magnet that draws the people, individually and collectively, unto itself.

The vision is *always powerful.* It assaults the sensitivities of the forest, flowing into depressions of human yearning, even if that yearning may be unconscious or denied. Once revealed, the person to whom it is revealed may feel intense inner turmoil, anxiety, and self-doubt. They may feel deeply inadequate or confused, fearful of the consequences either in turning toward or away from the vision. Nevertheless, the vision gradually overcomes all reservations. It communicates a kind of reckless courage. Ultimately, the individual recognizes that the vision is, indeed, a complete divine response that is absolutely appropriate to their yearning.

The vision is *always apocalyptic!* It may be unexpected, but it always provokes consternation. It is as if the ambiguities of human yearning, combining as they do selfless hope and selfish desire, confront that which is totally pure. The vision burns away selfishness. Individuals experiencing the vision may feel a loss, not unlike an addict experiences the pains of withdrawal. Yet the vision is inevitably surprising. It reveals a perspective on life and eternity that is entirely unimagined, and then sears it into the human heart so that it will forever be odd, out-of-step, and peculiar. With the passage of the vision, nothing is the same.

The vision appeals *to individuals!* The vision requires direct contact with the fullness of a human heart. Therefore, the vision does not seek to grasp committees, agencies, municipal governments or corporate organizations, or any other organized collection of people. Visions target persons. The vision does not simply linger in the shadows. It wafts its way through the forest. The vision singles out individuals and leaves them joyfully surprised, asking a question that can never be rationally answered: *Why me?*

The vision thrives *as a team vision!* The vision grows only through sharing. Its apocalyptic reality needs to be defined and refined through conversation. The conversation may sometimes be more exclamatory than propositional, or more poetic than prosaic. Indeed, the conversation may be entirely wordless, and yet profoundly communicative. Unless the vision becomes a team vision, it dies. The team vision is never hierarchical. Although there may be individuals who are the chief articulators of the vision, there is no single person who is the only expert about the vision. All have experienced it. All know it. All have equal authority and motivation to follow it. The vision will not be the individual. The vision lies beyond the individual and attracts a mighty following.

The vision only grows *among strangers!* The vision must leap into the unknown to be healthy. It motivates people to reach out beyond their circle of friendship. It beckons them to give birth to the potential within them. It continually risks rejection, for only then will all the nuances and facets of the vision become clear. People caught by the vision place themselves on a high learning curve, since the vision is always ahead of them. Every new friend who shares the vision teaches the others who have shared the vision earlier. The vision is never contained. It only expands.

Core Values

In addition to the core vision, the essence of the species will include clearly articulated core values. Again, the specific values, and unique articulation of values, will vary from organism to organism. They will always be oriented to the biblical description of the fruits of the Spirit: "love, joy, peace, patience, kindness, generosity, faithfulness, gentleness, and self-control" (Gal. 5:22). The essence of the species will touch upon the following key values:

- *Healthy relationships:* mutually enriching, respectful, affirming relationships that protect personal safety and correct dysfunctional leadership
- *Personal growth:* maturity, integrity, self-awareness, and balance in daily living
- *Multigenerational sensitivity:* empathy, empowerment, and health care for children and seniors
- *Generosity toward strangers:* respect for diversity, appreciation for differences without judgment, and acceptance of racial and gender equality and cultural uniqueness
- *Care for creation:* protection of the environment, enhancement of quality of life, and commitment to living in harmony with nature
- *Positive change:* confidence to embrace change, accepting of mystery, and taking risks in a context of mutual support
- *Eagerness to learn:* readiness to listen to, dialogue with, and learn from other perspectives.

Just as the authenticity of vision is verified in the joy, excitement, or motivation of the people, so also the authenticity of core values is verified in the daily behavior of the people. Participants in the Spiritual Redwood spontaneously mirror these values in workplace, neighborhood, and playground. The values are translated into behavioral standards, goals, or expectations for all activities within the Christian organism, no matter how trivial or profound.

Core Beliefs

In addition to core vision for motivation, and core values for behavior, the essence of the species will include clearly articulated core beliefs. These are the beliefs that inspire, inform, critique, and shape all strategic mapping, programming, and ministry. Spiritual Redwoods allow enormous scope for individual interpretations of doctrine, contextual perspectives in theology, and personal definitions of faith. At the same time, the core beliefs represent the consensus of the congregation beyond which one cannot venture without parting company with the organism. The essence of the species will touch on the following themes:

> **Core beliefs describe our experience with Jesus.**

- *Jesus as the immediacy of God's transforming power:* The daily walk with Jesus changes one's life and guides one's path.
- *God as an embracing, loving mystery:* The forgiveness and inclusivity of God's grace is constantly astonishing and manifest in countless ways.
- *The paradoxical destiny of the world of simultaneous acceptance and justice:* God's wisdom ensures both absolute justice over evil and absolute acceptance of weakness.
- *The Bible as authoritative, living Word:* Scripture both inspires and communicates the truth about life and death.
- *The gift and call of ministry for all Christians:* Every Christian is uniquely gifted and called by God into ministries that benefit others.
- *The assurance of fruitful daily living:* The hope for meaningful, purposeful, and fulfilling life is offered to every creature on earth.

The core beliefs that are the essence of the species may be articulated in many ways, and may bear many doctrinal interpretations. This is because they are not grounded in intellect, but rather in experience. They are always tentative, propositional descriptions of a common *experience* of God. In the end, it is not propositional agreement or dogmatic assent that binds the organism together, but the continuing touch of The Holy that is closely linked to their experience of the core vision. The authenticity of their commitment to these core beliefs will be verified in the quality and depth of their spiritual disciplines.

Mission!

Figure 5.5

The combination of core vision, core values, and core beliefs together lead the Spiritual Redwood into mission. The "mission statement" will bring together all three elements in a single, pithy, motivational expression of purpose. It is as if essential chemicals inside a rocket are mixed creating a volatile compound. It hisses, smokes, bubbles— and the rocket lifts off! In the same way, the mixture of core vision, values, and beliefs makes the Spiritual Redwood unstable. It cannot simply remain still. It must transfer its inherent energy to the surrounding forest. It must lift off into activity.

The explosive character of the mission of the Spiritual Redwood is due to the apocalyptic nature of its core vision. It transforms, changes, and redirects all of life. The goal-directed character of the mission of the Spiritual Redwood is due to its core values and beliefs. The explosion is aimed in specific directions, and released in specific ways. Simultaneously, the Spiritual Redwood releases power and meaning into the environment of the forest and transforms it. The missions of the Spiritual Redwood will be many,

The mission is to be and make disciples.

but the essential mission will always be the same: to be and to make disciples of Jesus!

Clifford and Elizabeth Pinchot have described the transformation of business organizations in their book *The End of Bureaucracy and the Rise of the Intelligent Organization*.[1] Their description of the bureaucratic structures that are disintegrating offers a parallel to the decline and fall of ecclesiastical machines. The nature of the machine is characterized by *central control* and *regimented activity:*

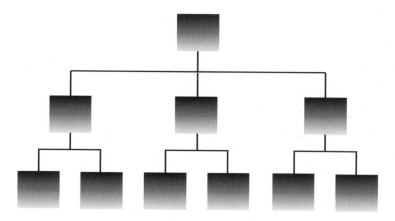

- hierarchical authority
- organizational divisions by offices or committees
- uniformity of rules or denominational polity
- standardized parliamentary or constitutional procedures
- seniority advancement in church management
- interaction through impersonal offices rather than personal relationships
- clergy authority and central coordination.

Such organizations worked well for a time, but no longer. The world has changed. Christendom has died. The Pinchots describe the transition for the business sector, which once again parallels the transition from ecclesiastical machines to Spiritual Redwoods. The nature of church work has changed:

1. Clifford and Elizabeth Pinchot, *The End of Bureaucracy and the Rise of the Intelligent Organization* (San Francisco: Berrett-Koehler Publishers, 1994), pp. 37, 55.

From	*To*
Unskilled obedience and fund-raising	Knowledgeable ministries
Repetitive management	Innovative initiative
Individual volunteerism	Team ministries
Generic programs	Specific projects
Limited skill for single tasks	Quality ministry, using multiple gifts
Authority of clergy	Authority of spiritually yearning people
Accountability to clergy	Accountability to peers

There was a time when machines, like bureaucracies, worked effectively. That era is now past, and the church is perhaps among the last cultural institutions to admit it.

The Inclinations of the Species

Let us repeat once again that the very nature of organic organizations prohibits any detailed description that can simply be replicated in every context with generally predictable results. The Spiritual Redwood is not a machine. On the other hand, just as we can describe what might be called the *essence* of the species, so also can we describe in broad terms the *inclinations* of the species. Spiritual Redwoods may do many different things, but they will do them in recognizable patterns.

The organizational machines of the institutional churches of the past all shared a basic philosophical orientation. They carved a "civilization" of Christendom out of the surrounding "forest" of culture. At first, the organization helped *advance* that civilization into the forest. Later, as the energies of Christendom waned and the nature of the forest itself changed, the organization *protected* Christendom from changing cultural forces. "Evangelism" and "Self-Preservation" were but two sides of the same organizational coin.

The inclination of the Spiritual Redwood is mutual trust, networks, and shared spiritual disciplines.

The pattern of church work was formed by an institutional consensus about the privileges and responsibilities of institutional membership. This consensus usually took the form of a summary of program, which was often wrongly considered to be a "mission statement." It was not. It was only a summation of various committee mandates of the church, and its real purpose was to inseparably link the bureaucracy of the institution with the organizational machine that advanced or preserved it. True "mission statements" translate the organizational essence of vision, values, and beliefs into dynamic action. These program summaries only clarified internal accountability. They motivated no action, changed nothing, and were quickly forgotten. This bureaucratic pattern of behavior can be summarized as follows:

Form a committee:
with a clear institutional mandate,
from selected recruits representing each special interest,
who are motivated by a strong sense of duty.
Locate them in parliamentary procedure.
Link them in perpetual, internal communication.
Accept the best that they can offer,
and supervise them constantly.

This pattern of church work assumed, and encouraged, an institutional membership that was homogeneous. Generally speaking, church participants looked remarkably alike. They shared the same racial, cultural, or language orientation. They lived in similar economic contexts. They came from similar professional or educational backgrounds. The organizational machine permitted enough diversity to "spice" the institutional consensus of the church, but never enough diversity to "change" the identity of the congregation.

Take a closer look at the inclination of ecclesiastical machines.

Form a committee . . . Action can only be taken through meetings led by chairpersons carefully appointed by the "central control" of the organizational machine. Administration and management are the spiritual gifts valued above all. The necessity of committee consensus strategically delays all decisions to allow time for emergency intervention from above. The real agent of the institution is not a "person," but an "office."

. . . *with a clear institutional mandate* . . . Each committee is provided with a prescriptive mandate that explicitly lists what the committee can or must do. The committee administers an approved program area of church life as defined in the mission statement. Innovation is not eliminated by the organizational machine, but it is controlled. And creativity that is controlled, is creativity that is discouraged.

. . . *from selected recruits representing each special interest* . . . Since the real servant of the institution is an "office," it is crucial that the officeholder be "representative." Nomination processes filter out troublesome or unduly creative candidates, and deliberately recruit individuals who do not speak for themselves, but do speak for a special interest group. Representatives of youth, women, men, racial or cultural minorities, physically or mentally challenged, and any other distinguishable group in the church will be recruited. Minorities in the community *beyond* the church, must first gain recognition as a group *within* the church, in order to be represented. Status as a recognized group requires initial accommodation to the homogeneity of the church.

. . . *who are motivated by a strong sense of duty.* . . . Since nomination to represent a group by serving an office assumes recognition within the church, committee members must have a strong sense of duty. Only "members" (no "adherents") can serve the organization. Their commitment is not simply to Christ, or to the universal church, but to this particular institution, its theological perspective and its religious practice, and to the organizational machine that preserves it. Committee members are tacitly pledged to advance or protect the organization. Behind this duty, there can be intense competition. Each represented group becomes a political faction seeking to influence or control the institutional agenda.

. . . *Locate them in parliamentary procedure.* . . . Since political acumen and competition ferment beneath the shared sense of duty, the church must locate each committee in parliamentary procedure. A detailed constitution defines the linear process of committee review and recommendation. The organizational machine allows the committee to do only what it is permitted to do, not what it wants to do. Committee members must know how to "work the system," a specialized knowledge which itself is another form of control. Gaining permission to do something that is not explicitly permitted in the committee mandate will require a combination of due process and appropriate patronage.

. . . Link them in perpetual, internal communication. . . . Since procedure and permission are necessary to accomplish even the smallest task, every unit must be in constant internal communication with every other unit in order to avoid intruding upon another's mandate. A representative from one committee must sit with another committee. The "liaison" task preoccupies the time and energy of volunteers, as each unit protects its area of responsibility. The serial connection of committees means that a single break in "liaison" activity can shut down the entire machine. Internal surveys become diagnostic checks to determine "where the system went wrong."

. . . Accept the best that they can offer . . . Since the "office" is surrounded by precise mandates and organizational process, the "officeholder" needs only to have a strong sense of duty. Talent, motivation, and calling are all secondary. The organizational machine is programmed in a "one size fits all" mode. Any person will do, so long as that person is representative. Indeed, officeholders easily rotate from one mandated committee to another. The organizational machine does not really want specific, content-related, mission expertise since this usually tests the boundaries of prescriptive committee mandates and becomes impatient with procedural delays. Little training beyond knowledge of how the machine works is needed. Volunteers just "do the best they can."

. . . and supervise them constantly. Since volunteers are just "doing their best," and since innovation is discouraged, the organizational machine is programmed with several redundant processes of supervision. The committee chairperson, the Board Executive, the Official Board itself, and the formal congregational meetings all do management. Every proposal or idea can be appealed. Every action is scrutinized several times. The organizational machine fears mistakes as much as it discourages innovation, since failure and creativity are linked together. Volunteers are supervised, not simply to protect them from embarrassment, but to protect the organization from the necessity of learning things from mistakes, which might change forever the organizational machine.

The organizational machines of the church institutions of Christendom are rapidly shutting down at the brink of the twenty-first century. They function in increasing disharmony with the changing culture around them. For all the talk about "growth" and "evangelism" in these organizations, the fact remains that they operate as adversaries to culture. "Growth" to these machines means only *membership* growth. "Evangelism" to these machines means only *assimilating the raw material of spiritual seekers into our homogeneous practice and perspective.* Culture beyond the church remains an enemy, toward which the church triumphantly advances, or from which the church self-righteously retreats.

Today, the Christendom supported by these organizational machines has perished. The forest has overwhelmed and buried them. They lie rusting amid the underbrush in various stages of operational decline. The creatures of the forest are either frightened by their odd noises and lights, or they stare curiously at them wondering what on earth *that thing does!*

Spiritual Redwoods, emerging to flourish in our pre-Christian era, have a completely different inclination. They are not machines. They are organisms at one with community. They may do many things, but they share a pattern of behavior.

The inclination of the species is formed by a growing, ever-changing team vision. The vision cannot be fully articulated in words, but emerges from the hearts of church participants in symbols and metaphors, and in dance and song. Their energy is not contained within an institutional box, but it seems to flow into them from the forest and the sky beyond. Visions are less predictable than mission statements. One cannot anticipate whether the wind that energizes the Spiritual Redwood will be strong or gentle, and one cannot predict with certainty what new directions the branches and roots of the tree might take. The inclination of the species can be summarized as follows:

Recognize a person:
with a clear awareness of spiritual gifts,
who is personally called by Jesus, and
who is motivated by a strong sense of destiny.
Anchor them in the core vision, values, beliefs, and mission of the organism.
Send them into a cascade of simultaneous ministries.
Equip them for excellence,
and get out of their way.

This pattern of activity assumes, and encourages, a living organism that is remarkably diverse. Generally speaking, church participants look and behave very different. They include many racial, cultural, and language orientations. They touch both the rich and the poor. They have many working and educational backgrounds—or no professional or educational identity at all. Spiritual Redwoods create an environment of safety, self-improvement, and hope.

Take a closer look at the inclination of Spiritual Redwoods:

Recognize a person . . . Action depends on personal initiative. The agent of mission is not an "office," but a person. This person is not recruited by the institution, but recognized as a gift from the Holy Spirit to the church and community. Persons "emerge" into mission based on the integrity and authenticity of their ministry, and the church must learn how they can support the mission to which an individual is called. They may "emerge" from within the church, or from the cultural forest beyond the church. Spiritual Redwoods take time to understand the unique personhood of each individual, and readjust their own structures to augment that person's growth.

> **Spiritual Redwoods love people more than committees or procedures.**

. . . with a clear awareness of spiritual gifts . . . Personal growth begins with a clear awareness of the array of spiritual gifts God has given to the individual. The church creates a climate or process in which individuals can perceive clearly these gifts, the exercise of which will fulfill the mission of Jesus and the life of the individual. Instead of a "prescriptive" mandate, the church provides the gifted individual with a proscriptive boundary within which their innovative energies can be released.

. . . who is personally called by Jesus, and . . . Since recognized persons in mission are expected to be innovative, they must be personally passionate about their mission. Their goal is not to represent a subculture, but to represent Jesus amid multiple subcultures. They are individually the spiritual descendants of Moses and Miriam, with all the passion and unpredictability of the biblical saints. The institutional "machines" of Christendom had a clearly defined

"production" goal (i.e., specific programs, liturgies, and advocacies), but the Spiritual Redwood in the pre-Christian era only knows that it is changing and growing. The mission agenda emerges from the multiple callings of persons in their midst.

. . . *who is motivated by a strong sense of destiny.* . . . Since the mission agenda emerges from the callings of individuals, and not from a "Central Control" in the "machine," persons are motivated primarily by a sense of their own destiny. The fulfillment of the mission of Jesus, and the fulfillment of one's own created purpose, are one. They are "branches grafted onto the True Vine," and flourish only in that unity. They are "body parts" functioning as they were created to function, in harmony with the whole Body of Christ. The competitive politics of the organizational "machine" vanish. Enthusiastic support for the Spiritual Redwood is based upon the liberty each part is given to become all God has destined it to be.

. . . *Anchor them in the core vision, values, beliefs, and mission of the organism.* . . . The core vision, values, beliefs, and mission of the organism function like a genetic code that marks each cell of the Spiritual Redwood. They do not need to be located in parlia mentary procedure, because they do not need to be controlled. And they do not need to be controlled, because they spontaneously and automatically live within the core identity of the Spiritual Redwood. They are free to grow, create, or be whatever they choose.

. . . *Send them into a cascade of simultaneous ministries.* . . . "Discovering what works in a particular universe of any organization is the task of everyone in that organization" (Margaret Wheatley, *A Simpler Way*). While redundancy may be failure to a machine, it is a celebration of life to the Spiritual Redwood. The same issue can be addressed from any number of perspectives, and the same method can result in any number of positive outcomes. There is never just one way. Innovations multiply, parallel one another, cross over one another, and expand upon one another. "Liaison" is a waste of time. Priority in listening is not an internal necessity to the organization, but only an external necessity to discern the changing needs and yearnings of the forest. Such a cascade of simultaneous ministries may seem chaotic, but, as Wheatley says, "Fuzzy, messy, continuously exploring systems bent on discovering what works are far more practical and successful than our attempts at efficiency."[2] The cumulative impact of multiple and even redundant ministries is more powerful than any single action.

. . . *Equip them for excellence* . . . Since the purpose of networking is not approval and control, but sharing and learning, the church cannot simply accept the best individuals can offer. The church must help individuals *do better!* The Spiritual Redwood can only thrive if every unit within it is striving to grow higher, reach farther, burrow deeper, and flutter in the breeze of the Holy Spirit with ever more beauty. The quality of skill, the breadth of knowledge, and the depth of spirituality are all unending quests. The authority to be in mission is not granted, but gained. Integrity comes first.

. . . *and get out of their way.* Since the Spiritual Redwood builds integrity, and does not merely disperse authority, a climate of trust permeates the church. Trust implies mutual accountability, but it does not imply linear control. If persons are equipped for excellence, continued institutional meddling will only frustrate innovation and mission effectiveness. Spiritual Redwoods do not fear mistakes. They welcome mistakes, because they have equipped persons to learn from them.

Spiritual Redwoods thrive because they are serious about growing people.

Spiritual Redwoods thrive in the forest of the contemporary pre-Christian era because they are serious about growth. The goal is not to provide a little shade for whatever woodland creature chooses to seek refuge underneath their branches, but to provide *ever larger and safer shade* for creatures hitherto indifferent to the tree. The Christian organism creates an environment within the forest of hospitality, safety, enlightenment, peace, and mutually respectful communication. The Spiritual Redwood does not need to protect itself from the "forest" of culture, but knows itself to be a part of culture. The Spiritual Redwood does not need to advance itself, but seeks only to help the many persons within it to advance themselves.

Spiritual Redwoods will grow in infinite varieties, but the inclination of the species will always be toward certain patterns of activity. Three distinct themes can be discerned from the contrasts just described.

---

2. Margaret Wheatley, *A Simpler Way* (San Francisco: Berrett-Koehler Publishers, 1996).

Linear Accountability Versus Mutual Trust

Machines always function in certain ways, no matter how sophisticated they might be. Whether or not one imagines organizational structures to be "triangular" autocracies, or "inverted triangular" democracies, lines of accountability and parliamentary procedure dominate the model of the institutional church. No matter how much the hierarchy is flattened, there are still two kinds of people within the organization: *Initiators-Evaluators* and *Doers*. Their interaction is described in the following diagram:

Method for Machines

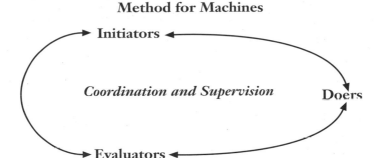

Initiators

Coordination and Supervision   Doers

Evaluators

Figure 5.6

A central control of clergy and lay officers defines the priorities for action of the church ("mission agenda"). They recruit volunteers to implement those priorities. These "Doers" of work are closely supervised, and their performance in implementing institutional priorities is carefully evaluated.

However complex the organizational structure becomes, this simple strategy is always assumed. To be sure, "Initiators" seek to persuade "Doers" to take ownership of the priorities for action. Their advice might be annually sought as the Initiators deliberate, and the commitment of those who volunteer will be genuine. Doers truly share enthusiasm for the work. It would be an overstatement, however, to say that Doers truly "own" the work.

First, the perpetual motion of the institutional machine ensures that the advice of Doers never strays far from the wisdom of Initiators. The distribution of most congregational surveys, for example, is limited to those already attending worship or known to be already active in the church. Annual meetings are designed to emphasize management, rather than vision.

Second, the recruitment process for Doers ensures that those not in agreement with the priorities for action do not have a chance to "do" anything at all. The fact that institutional machines perpetually discharged a "waste product" of inactive members reveals that ownership by Doers is more propaganda than reality.

Doers can fine-tune the institutional agenda, but they must agree with the agenda ultimately decided by the Initiators. Those who do not agree become "Non-Doers," whose advice will no longer be invited.

In the Spiritual Redwood, everyone can initiate, evaluate, and do ministry.

The power to "initiate" and the power to "evaluate" are the same power. Those who initiate priorities for action, and those who evaluate performance to fulfill those priorities are the same people. An appearance of division of labor might be offered within the institution, but ultimately the same people gave or withheld permission. Change comes slowly, as Doers are carefully screened and promoted to become Initiators and Evaluators. The "perpetual motion"—repeatability, consistency, and predictability—of the "machine" is

Method for Organisms

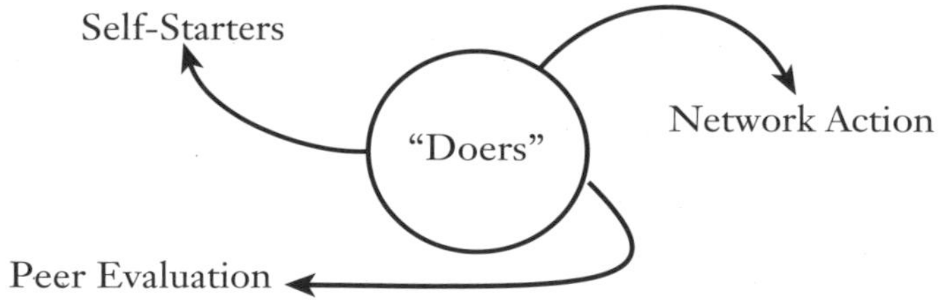

Self-Starters

"Doers"

Network Action

Peer Evaluation

Figure 5.7

valued more than anything else. The most commonly expressed anxiety is that things might "get out of hand," or that the church might "get out of control."

Spiritual Redwoods are naturally inclined to reject linear

accountability in favor of mutual trust. The powers to initiate, implement, and evaluate are shared equally by every participant in the spiritual organism. Their interaction is described in figure 5.7. Each person shares these elemental responsibilities. Mission design, power to act, and quest for quality are built into every part of the organism. Essentially, there is only one kind of participant in the Spiritual Redwood: the Doer.

Volunteers in the Spiritual Redwood are "self-initiators." Each person sets a personal mission priority. They are not recruited by a central control to perform institutional tasks, but they are motivated by a sense of their own calling by God to perform significant ministry. The same individual has the united power to *design* and to *implement* ministry. Their purpose is not to envision a ministry and persuade others to do it; nor is their purpose to do a ministry that others have envisioned and planned. They do both together.

Volunteers in the Spiritual Redwood are "networked" into ever-changing teams. They do not join a fixed committee bound by a prescriptive mandate, but they find people who share their enthusiasm and together design and implement ministry with proscribed boundaries of belief and values. These boundaries are the core values, beliefs, vision, and mission, beyond which no ministry can go, but within which any ministry can begin, grow, and evolve in any way imaginable. As projects change and evolve, so also do the teams change and evolve. More than this, ministry teams constantly trade information with one another. They are constantly seeking opportunities for a creative connection of ministry hitherto unexpected or unknown. New and timely partnerships are always emerging.

Volunteers in the Spiritual Redwood are committed to excellence and rely on peer evaluation. They are not evaluated by a central control on the basis of their performance in implementing the mission set by others; they evaluate one another on the basis of the quality with which they are implementing their shared mission. *Am I learning and growing? Can this ministry be done even better? Are there opportunities that can be pursued harder? Have I gone beyond the boundary of beliefs and values that identify the Spiritual Redwood?*

The linear accountability of the institutional "machines" of Christendom is a chain of simultaneous reporting and supervision. The larger and more complex the machine becomes, the more that decision making becomes redundant. Additional "back-up" systems safeguard the machine from unauthorized activities. The machine responds to every leadership crisis by creating another layer of supervision or a new policy, and responds to every volunteer mistake by creating another level of bureaucracy. In the end, even the smallest activity requires extensive permission. These institutional "machines" cannot adapt quickly enough to the encroaching "forest" of North American culture. The machine expends enormous energy, with remarkably small output.

Spiritual Redwoods surround lateral thinking with well-articulated values and beliefs. They create an environment of instant decision and constant creativity, based on mutual trust. Performance is not reviewed from beyond the individual, but from within the individual. The review is not periodic, but constant. And the commitment to quality is not imposed from beyond the specific mission field, but pursued within the specific mission field. In the end, even the most ambitious ministry can be implemented quickly. The Spiritual Redwood adapts to the "forest" of North American culture. The Spiritual Redwood expends the same energy, but with proportionate productivity.

Middle Management Versus Web of Communication

In ecclesiastical machines, the linear connection between Initiators-Evaluators and Doers implies not only complex structures of accountability and control, but multiple layers of coordination. The institutional machines of Christendom require extensive "middle management." Between the clergy and controlling lay leaders, and those who implement the mission of the institution, countless volunteers devote energy to management and administration. More people are involved in management than ministry. They are the chain of simultaneous reporting and supervision. Committee chairpersons, vice-chairpersons, and secretaries; group presidents, vice-presidents, and program officers; trustees, treasurers, and membership recorders—all these "offices" are required to keep the "machine" running. They recruit the Doers, who implement the institutional mission agenda. They monitor the activities of the Doers, process their reports, and intervene when they get into trouble.

As long as initiation-evaluation and implementation are separated, middle management will be crucial to the institution. As long as "control" is the primary institutional priority, bureaucracy will inevitably grow. There will be more and more reports, more and more meetings, and more and more offices. Some middle management positions (e.g., Youth Workers, Church Administrators, Social Advocates) will be salaried, but most will be volunteer. Leadership "burnout" becomes a greater and greater threat to the machine:

- because the church cannot afford many salaried middle managers
- because fewer and fewer people find middle management fulfilling
- because bureaucratic work always increases, while the available pool of willing volunteers steadily decreases
- because volunteers must serve multiple offices.

When leadership burnout among middle management becomes extreme, the institutional machine short-circuits. "Sparks" of conflict shoot from the mechanism of church life.

One preferred solution has been to "downsize." Salaried "middle management" positions are terminated. Committees and offices are consolidated. Meetings, and the duration of meetings, become even more tightly controlled. Unfortunately, mere downsizing ultimately does not work. The institutional machine is what it is. It cannot function without middle management. The system does not run smoothly, and delays and gaps appear in institutional life. That remarkably small output of the machine proves to be the most vulnerable aspect of institutional life, so that the institution has less and less connection with daily affairs beyond the membership. Real ministry, which reaches out beyond the institution, all but disappears. Inevitably bureaucracy rises again.

The other preferred solution is to "automate." This partly means that the church invests money to upgrade office machinery, worship equipment, and telephone communications. This allows the church to trim salaried support-staff positions to part-time, and transform routine work into automatic processes. Mostly, however, "automation" for the church means establishing additional policies and operating procedures. More and more

Redwoods share information.

work happens "automatically" in the church without thought to the ambiguities of personal context. Unfortunately, "automation" strips the institutional church of its "personable" veneer and makes it look even more like a machine.

Of course, "control" is the very essence of a "machine." That control may be adjusted, modified, relaxed, or tightened, *but it is never relinquished!* If it is relinquished, the very essence of the institutional church of Christendom is lost.

Spiritual Redwoods relinquish most control. Therefore, middle management can be replaced by a "Web of Communication." The key to ministry is not coordination and administration, but the sharing of information and ideas. Individuals need a rapid and effective communications system through which:

- they can learn and refine their sense of calling
- they can deepen their knowledge and upgrade their skills
- they can locate others who share their enthusiasm
- they can build partnerships with others where enthusiasms intersect.

This web of communication is easily accessible and easily used. One does not need to serve an office, nor does one need extensive training. Spiritual Redwoods multiply the ways in which one part of the organism can instantly communicate with another part of the organism, without having to go through intermediaries either for permission, or for the expert guidance that is simply another means of control.

Spiritual Redwoods are attuned to the "information" revolution that has changed North American culture. They do not try to censor or control the information that is allowed to be consumed by the participants of the church. To borrow a word from the Pinchots, they are truly an "intr*a*net" for spiritual travelers, in which users behave with a protocol similar to that described by America On-line:

- Be respectful.
- Be kind.
- Refrain from selling products or coercing others.
- Give, don't just receive.
- Never give up.
- Celebrate the enormous mystery of imagination and truth.

Spiritual Redwoods help participants know how to gather accurate information, assess information for relevance and value, and use information to design effective ministry. They provide twenty-four-hour support for every cell of the tree that is spiritually "on-line."

As the distinction between Initiators-Evaluators and Doers disappears, the coordinating responsibilities of middle management are absorbed by the Doers themselves. In part, this is possible because the spiritual organism invests heavily in technology that can instantly and constantly link the parts of the Body of Christ together. "Modems" have replaced "Meetings." In part this is possible because Doers have become entrepreneurs with an internalized motivation for excellence. "Membership Obedience" has been replaced by "Ministry Skill." And in part this is possible because organizational culture has become open to change. "Preservation" has been replaced by "Experimentation."

Reciprocal Rewards Versus Shared Spiritual Discipline

The preoccupation with "control" by the institutional "machines" of Christendom emphasizes *product* and *process*. To some extent, the decades of battle between the "conservative" and "liberal" churches of Christendom were all about the prioritizing of these two aspects of control. Control of *product* usually implied targets like:

- the number of "converts" in the community
- the amount of money given to charity
- the number of new "members" in the church
- the number of signatures on petitions, people on marches, or prophets in protest
- the quantity of programs linked to the church.

Control of *process* usually implied targets like:

- the number of people involved in decision making
- the ability to use parliamentary procedure
- the effectiveness of committees in achieving bureaucratic consensus
- the preservation of institutional continuity
- the success of nominations processes.

Although the priority of these two aspects of control has been disputed within Christendom, both forms of control have been central to Christendom.

Control is not only exercised by separating the powers to initiate and to implement, but by creating an organizational ethos of reciprocal rewards. People participate in the institution because they can receive specific benefits from membership, and the institution recruits participation because preservation of the corporate structure and goals can be perpetuated.

"If you do that for the institution, the institution will do this for you." Members give time, energy, and money to the institution. In return, they will be rewarded with certain privileges. For example, they will not be charged any fees for weddings and funerals, they will have immediate access to the minister day or night, they can expect the visits and prayers of others when in the hospital, they can expect to receive praise in public. People join the church with a view to what membership benefits can be gained.

"If the institution does this for you, it has the right to expect you will do that for the institution." The services provided by the institutional church are rewarded with increased financial support, volunteer energy for committees, and commitment to maintaining heritage and property. People are welcomed into the church with a view to what they can offer the institutional agenda.

This system of reciprocal rewards brings the Initiators-Evaluators and the Doers into an unhealthy codependency. Management is always seeking to "recruit" members, and seekers only join because they "want" something from management. Their relationship is akin to that between "employer" and "employee." People are "hired" into the corporate organization with the expectation of receiving "benefits"; if they do not perform well, they are "let go" by the organization and must pay for services like everyone else.

In the past, the degree of control exercised by the institutional church over product and process, determined the "cost" of membership. If the benefits of membership were not commensurate with the demands of membership, people would leave. The institution would either reduce its expectations, or redefine its self-image. For example, if institutional demands for money were too constant or too high, or demands for time to attend meetings unrealistic, church participants would drop out. They would become Non-Doers and lose influence in the institutional machine. The church would either re-

Membership entitlements are over.

duce expectations of financial and meeting support, or redefine its identity to become a "righteous remnant" of "true believers" for which small size was a spiritual vindication.

On the brink of the twenty-first century, however, the reemergence of the pre-Christian era has changed forever this system of reciprocal rewards. "Control" can no longer simply be adjusted. The very fact of institutional "control" is now in itself too high a price to pay for the benefits of institutional membership. The very separation of Initiators-Evaluators and Doers is no longer acceptable. People neither wish to be managed, nor do they wish to manage others. They yearn for trusted independence. They yearn to participate in a network of mutually respectful, mutually helpful spiritual travelers.

Spiritual Redwoods relinquish control, by replacing the system of reciprocal rewards with *shared spiritual discipline*. These spiritual disciplines are of several kinds.

First, every individual separately pursues disciplines of prayer and Bible reading. Each individual trusts that others are pursuing the same discipline. They may not know what others are praying or reading. They may not know what others are thinking, or what conclusions about faith and daily living they are drawing. They simply believe that the same Holy Spirit is working with every individual through this independent discipline.

Second, every individual is linked to a small group in which prayer and Bible reading are shared, and in which honest conversation seeks to discern how faith can change and direct daily living. They may not always agree with one another, but they are confident that they can learn from one another. They believe the Holy Spirit is in their midst.

Third, every individual is linked to the larger organism of the Spiritual Redwood. The small group may be all "roots," all "branches," all "bark," or all "leaves." It may also be a mix of every conceivable cell of the tree. More than this, the spiritual discipline of the Spiritual Redwood beckons every person to regular worship, every week, fifty-two weeks out of the year, with no holidays to the cottage or the beach. These are times of coaching, inspiration, gratitude—and continuing life change.

Fourth, all individuals seriously endeavor to engage their faith with daily living, through constant attention to their mission. They seriously plan their day seeking to live and share the beliefs and values they hold dear. This alters their behavior patterns in the home, the workplace, and the playground.

None of these disciplines is easy. They may encounter opposition (active or benign) from spouses, family members, work associates, neighbors, and friends. Coaching, mutual support, and inspirational worship keep them motivated. Each person will likely add disciplines or "helps" to keep themselves on track. Incentive to continue comes partly through the shared evidence of positive change within and beyond themselves, but mostly from their own sense of joy in doing what they are destined to do.

Control of product and process is replaced by a spiritual synergy. Each part of the Spiritual Redwood "cheers on" the other parts, and each part devotes energy to the success of the other parts. The web of constant, instant networking creates an environment of open, sincere, and absolutely honest sharing. Mutual Trust generates a readiness to listen and learn.

"Control" of a machine is replaced by "nurture" of a living organism. Spiritual Redwoods do not control the processes of organization, but allow enormous spontaneity and originality and "feed" all parts of the organism with basic beliefs and values. Again, Spiritual Redwoods do not control the products of organization, but allow an enormous diversity of ministries to blossom forth and integrate these ministries into a long-range plan of health, safety, and spiritual depth for the community and the world. Spiritual Redwoods create a synergy uniquely their own, through the provision of food for faith—and a long-term vision to transform the "forest" into the "Garden of Eden."

Spiritual Redwoods are the tallest trees in the forest, and yet they have no primary aim to grow at all! Growth is a secondary benefit, a kind of organic by-product, of the synergy they create. The goal of the Spiritual Redwood is for each root, each twig, each leaf, each blossom to achieve its full potential. Only when each part of the organism flourishes has the Spiritual Redwood fulfilled its purpose. Does the Spiritual Redwood have

Control is replaced with nurture.

one hundred members, or ten thousand members? Are there twenty in a single weekly worship service, or fifteen thousand in multiple weekly worship services? None of this matters. The only thing that matters is that each tiny cell of the organism live to its full potential.

The Fruits of the Species

What a huge contrast there is between the institutional church "machines" of Christendom that now go to rust and ruin in the midst of the forest of North American culture, and the Christian organisms called "Spiritual Redwoods" that thrive in the midst of that same forest! The essence and inclination of the species are radically different. They have an aroma or scent that is harder to identify, but infinitely more pleasing than the oily odor of a machine at work. They have a pattern of behavior that is remarkably diverse, but infinitely more attractive than the whirring and whining of the ecclesiastical machine.

It is no surprise, therefore, that Spiritual Redwoods bear very different fruits, which are ingested into the experience of the entire forest.

The Essence of the Species

Core Vision

Machines	Spiritual Redwoods
Historical creeds	Compass orientation
Committee mandates	Songs of the heart
Membership	Calling
Maintenance	Transformation

Core Values

Machines	Spiritual Redwoods
Friendship	Love
Contentment	Joy
Agreement	Peace
Pastoral care	Universal kindness
Diplomacy	Generosity
Allegiance	Faithfulness
Factional competition	Gentleness
Supervision	Self-control

Core Beliefs

Machines	Spiritual Redwoods
Dogmatic catechisms	Daily life with Jesus
Obedience to unintelligible deity	Celebration of mysterious love
Fear of either-or judgment	Confidence in unity of acceptance and justice
Power of personality or perspective	Pervasive influence of Scripture
Sunday Christian living	Seven-day-a-week Christian living

Core Mission

Machines	Spiritual Redwoods
Program summaries	Motivational mission statements
Denominational mission funds	Congregational mission activities
Mission agendas from above	Mission opportunities from below

The Inclination of the Species

Machines	Spiritual Redwoods
Hierarchical authority	Individual initiative
Increasing bureaucracy	Instant permission
Uniform rules	Customized contextual tactics
Standardized procedures	Creative strategies
Multiple church managers	Multiple ministers
Impersonal offices	Personal midwives
Clergy authority	Laity authority

"Machines" and "living organisms" are qualitatively different. They are complex systems that produce very different outcomes. Machines cannot produce the outcomes of a living organism, and living organisms cannot produce the outcomes of a machine. It may be that a machine can be painted green, decorated in floral patterns, and scented with cherry blossoms—and that this might be done so cleverly that a casual observer might think it is actually alive. A Spiritual Redwood may be quite plain. The "bark" may be ordinary brick, the "roots" may be ordinary people, and the "branches" appear to be ordinary charita-

Figure 5.8: Seeds for New Life

ble projects. Yet closer observation reveals the truth.

Although the ministries of a Spiritual Redwood are released in chaotic cascades of mission, in which internal liaison is secondary to creative action, the roots of the Spiritual Redwood network together. In fact, they become intertwined with the roots of other Spiritual Redwoods in a web of constant communication and mutual support. They bear fruits of cooperation, rather than competition. They grow best in "groves," rather than individually. Their vast networks of learning anchor the entire soil system of the forest.

The fact is that the fruits of the Spiritual Redwood are ingested by the ecosystem of the forest. These fruits create a healthier environment of Christian faith, community values, and long-term confidence for the future. Ecclesiastical machines leave a community legacy of religious competition, power struggle, and disillusionment with bureaucracy. The fruits of the Spiritual Redwood plant seeds in the community that augment individual freedoms and community responsibility. Ecclesiastical machines leave a community legacy of polarization between "insiders" and "outsiders," and an adversarial struggle between the sacred and the secular. The fruits of the Spiritual Redwood blossom into an environment of greater equality and respect, greater opportunity for growth and experimentation, and greater safety in personal relationships.

Ye shall know them by their fruits . . .

VISTA SIX

A Chaos of Vitality

Cellular Structure and Leadership

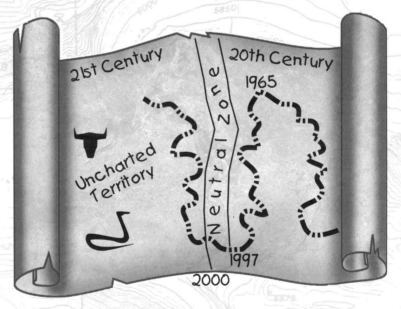

To develop lay
pastors, small groups,
and team ministries, lay a solid
foundation.

O bserve the giant redwood standing in the forest. At first glance, it seems but another object among a forest of objects. It might be a rock, or a stone . . . or a particularly complex machine. Then the presence of the redwood washes over the observer's sensitivities. The aroma conveys the peculiar essence of the species. The colors are many, changing, and subtle. Movements among the branches, visible and hidden, reveal a riot of diversity. Roots that are partially revealed above ground suggest a depth of significance as yet to be revealed. Despite the variety of leaf and branch, one senses an inclination or purposefulness about its existence. Its fruits and seeds seem to feed the health and well-being of the forest surrounding it. It is not awake and active one day a week. It is teeming with purpose and activity twenty-four hours a day. The creatures of the forest come and go from within its branches. The conclusions come spontaneously to the mind of the observer: "There is safety here. There is health here. There is growth here. There is life here."

The surest signs of life, however, are discovered not by observation, but by participation. Once enter into the life of the redwood, and one discovers the real reason for its vibrant life. There is unity, yet there is incredible diversity. There is continuity, yet there is constant surprise. Why? Because the redwood is itself a "self-starter," which nurtures individual initiative. Initiative, entrepreneurship, creativity, and change are the stuff of life.

On the one hand, every branch, twig, or leaf, and every root, vine, or tendril, is free to find its own way. If there is an obstacle in the way of growth—boulder, cliff, or rusted metal—each part of the organism can customize its own route of growth to overcome that obstacle. Each part of the redwood, no matter how small, is a microcosm of freedom. On the other hand, each part of the organism is networked with every other part. If in its growth and movement it encounters some danger, or discerns some opportunity, the news is instantly conveyed to every other part of the organism, so that every part of the organism can prepare itself for good or ill.

On the one hand, every fruit and every seed, no matter how different in design or appearance, affects the life of the forest in its own way. The redwood is a resource of food and shelter, work and play, learning and growth. Together the many fruits and seeds provide a veritable banquet of choices to suit every taste and address every need. Each fruit and seed is a microcosm of individuality. On the other hand, each seed and fruit infuses into the forest the same fundamental meaning that is the essence *of the species. The seedlings that grow are redwoods also. The fruits that are ingested by the forest infuse each creature with the essence of redwood. Even crisis and tragedy reveal the "self-starting" nature of the redwood. Lightning, fire, flood, or earthquake may break off branches, or even cause the tree to collapse. And yet it does not die! It does not die, because each unit of the organism, even the smallest cell of the organism, is a "self-starter." The broken branch takes root. A shoot of green arising from the stump signals the resurrection of the Spiritual Redwood. It grows again. It keeps coming back. Its vitality cannot be checked. It is born to grow, and grows to be reborn.*

Spiritual Redwoods are "self-starting" organisms that nurture initiative in every part of the organism. Each individual, team, or group of the Body of Christ is a microcosm of freedom. They can consider any option, design any plan, and implement any activity immediately and without middle management. At the same time, each part of the organism is linked to the other parts of the organism by networks of learning and communication.

Similarly, each initiative, mission, or ministry of the Body of Christ is part of a larger banquet of choices for the public. It can adjust its content in any way, deliver its message in any form, and conduct its business in any style without hindrance or threat of judgment. At the same time, each part of the organism communicates the same fundamental vision, beliefs, and values that are the essence of the species.

"Self-starting" organisms that nurture initiative survive crisis or tragedy. A few years ago, an airplane carrying top American business executives on a trade mission to the Balkans crashed. Immediately, several top corporations were brought to the brink of imminent collapse. In the same way, the ecclesiastical machines of the past could collapse simply by the death or retirement of their key clergy. Such "bureaucracies" or "machines" break down when there is a threat to their central control. "Self-starting" organisms, however, have decentralized authority and dispersed power to all their parts. More than this, each part carries within itself the essence of the whole. It is not just *power* that has been dispersed and shared, but also *meaning and purpose* that has been dispersed and shared. Therefore, neither the loss of a key leader, nor the fire that destroys a church building, nor the shift in culture that contradicts the effectiveness of a particular style of ministry, can ultimately destroy the organism. A shoot grows from the stump—and it is reborn to thrive again.

It is this "self-starting" nature of Spiritual Redwoods that sets them apart from past organizations. Each cell carries within itself the power and meaning to replicate the whole all over again. Christian leaders must ask themselves: *If anything happened to destroy this Body of Christ, such that all that was left was a single "twig" or "small group," could that small unit thrive on its own? Could it grow again? Could it replicate the essence of the Body of Christ that was lost?*

Each cell has the ability to replicate the whole.

"Self-starting" organisms have a penchant for resurrection. In a sense, the Spiritual Redwood is not even like a human body. Cut off a finger or an ear, and that finger or ear will not be able to regenerate an entire body. The Spiritual Redwood is a multicelled, multi-empowered organism. Cut off a single cell, and that single cell can thrive on its own and eventually multiply into an organism that once again reflects the essence of the species. Each part contains within itself the power and meaning of the whole.

In various places, we have described these diverse, empowered, "meaning-bearing" units of the Spiritual Redwood as small groups ("L.I.F.E. Groups," "P.A.L.S. Groups"), affinity groups ("discovery" groups, "destiny groups"), or teams ("ministry teams," "administration teams"). In the corporate business sector, Gifford and Elizabeth Pinchot, in their book *The End of Bureaucracy and the Rise of the Intelligent Organization*, have coined the term "free intraprises" to describe such units.[1] They argue that such units of "free intraprise" characterize the intelligent organization that is replacing bureaucracies, and that each unit balances within itself freedom of choice and responsibility for the whole.

We believe that Spiritual Redwoods are living organisms composed of many organic "cells." These cells may be simple or complex. They may be individuals, teams, groups, or even larger networks. They may interact in diverse ways and form periodic partnerships for specific tasks. Each cell is distinct. It carries within itself its own power of self-determination and is not subject to any other cell. At the same time, each cell contains within itself the imprint of the whole and perpetually seeks the well-being of every other cell. In Christian reference, each cell balances *Freedom* and *Covenant*.

---

1. Gifford and Elizabeth Pinchot, *The End of Bureaucracy and the Rise of the Intelligent Organization* (San Francisco: Berrett-Koehler, 1994), pp. 63ff.

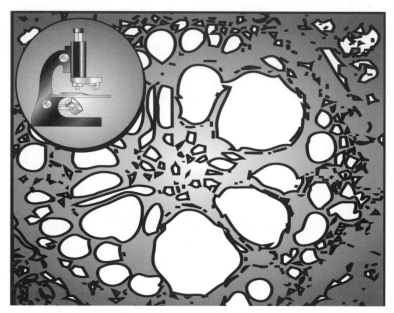

Figure 6.1: Spiritual Redwood Cell Structure

Freedom	*Covenant*
The freedom to think, speak, and consult	Relationships of affirmation and acceptance
The power to imagine, decide, and act	Networks of learning and cooperation
The ability to share, care, and critique.	Webs of equal voice, shared values, and common purpose.

Within the core vision, core beliefs, and core values, which alone define the "essence of the species," the many cells of the organism thrive in innumerable ways. Behind the appearance of placidity and sturdiness that first strikes the outside observer, there lies a veritable chaos of individuality and initiative. Yet the Spiritual Redwood nurtures every cell to balance freedom and covenant. The maximum of creativity, and the maximum of benevolence, are simultaneously encouraged.

The freedom to think, speak, and consult. Each cell is free to discover God, interpret scriptures, define doctrines, and develop ideas as they wish. They may disagree with the ideas of other cells, but that is acceptable. They are free to speak their minds honestly, without fear of punishment. They are free to seek the advice of anyone within or beyond the church, read whatever resources they may find useful, or participate in any experience that helps them to grow in healthy relationships or deepen their faith. There is never any explicit, or implicit, censorship.

The power to imagine, decide, and act. Each cell has full power to interpret the needs and yearnings of people within and beyond the church, and to design creative plans for mission or ministry. They have complete power to decide what to do, when to do it, and how to do it. They can act without any approvals from a central authority, accepting for themselves the risks of failure and the joys of success. There is never a need for middle management.

The ability to share, care, and critique. Each cell creates a climate of safety and mutual respect that allows participants to share with honesty and the assurance of confidentiality. The participants care as much about one another, as they do about their activities and missions. Mutual, constructive criticism is encouraged, as all participants place themselves on the highest learning curve possible. There is never a need for hierarchical supervision.

Relationships of affirmation and acceptance. What balances the freedom of the cell is the covenant of the cell to build quality relationships with all participants in the Spiritual Redwood. They are committed to conversation, rather than confrontation. They recognize the equality in which no single cell has power to control other cells. They affirm uniqueness and originality; value diversity of perspective, taste, and lifestyle; and accept people as they are, rather than as they might be used. Both prejudice and patronage are perpetually rejected.

Networks of learning and cooperation. What balances the power of the cell is the covenant of the cell to deepen faith in a shared quest for integrity and quality. The risks of imagination and action are balanced by the disciplines to learn from both success and failure. The high learning curve within each cell is accelerated and broadened through communication, scriptural study, and theological reflection. Cells synthesize information from many diverse sources from the cultural forest. Narrow-mindedness and mediocrity are systematically eliminated.

Each cell has a genetic code of faith, learning, mission, and caring.

Webs of equal voice, shared values, and common purpose. What balances the ability for honest critique within each cell is the covenant of the cell to extend the same respect to other cells of the Spiritual Redwood. They share together the continuing process of defining, refining, and celebrating the core vision, beliefs, values, and mission, which together are the essence of the species. They enter constantly evolving and changing partnerships to augment effectiveness and excellence in ministry. Dictatorial behavior and dogmatism are consistently discarded.

Spiritual Redwoods nurture this balance of freedom and covenant by imprinting a "genetic code" of faith, learning, mission, and caring assumptions in each cell. In a sense, this is the "minimal governance" (of which the Pinchots speak) that is needed to harness the chaos of cellular life into the true creative harmony of the Spiritual Redwood. This imprint allows all that creative, *entre*preneurial and *intra*preneurial, behavior to nevertheless appear to the outside observer as a single, placid, sturdy, vibrant tree.

Faith Assumptions
Any profound experience of faith must include:

a. *An experience of the Holy that questions, deepens, changes, and enriches.* God's power needs to be felt in the heart, in order to change the motivation and behavior of individuals. It needs to enrich one's life, and open one to mystery. It needs to invite constant questioning and dialogue, and allow one to interpret for oneself who this God is, and what this God is doing with one's life.

b. *An experience of deep, healthy relationships with partners on a journey.* Faith development needs quality intimacy with people who share one's desire for God. Mutual support, honesty, respect, and prayer help people find their way through ambiguity.

c. *An experience of self-discovery and maturing self-esteem.* Faith development needs a foundation of positive self-worth, and a readiness to discover whatever lies hidden within oneself. It requires confidence that beneath all the vices and failings, there is a person who is essentially lovable.

d. *An experience of deep, sensitive compassion for strangers.* Spiritual growth deepens when one's attention transcends self to recognize the needs and yearnings of others. Faith and hospitality to strangers are two sides of the same coin.

e. *An experience of humility, growth, and celebration.* Enduring faith confronts all obstacles with hope. One must always be open to learning new things and playing diverse personal roles. Thanksgiving and celebration lie at the heart of a deep faith.

Learning Assumptions
Profound personal growth requires:

a. *Learning through intimate, challenging, and informed conversation.* Dialogue that is honest and knowledgeable helps every participant form interpretations of the world with integrity and respect.

b. *Learning through problem solving and development of practical life skills.* Growth begins by addressing pressing issues and questions, and equips individuals to overcome obstacles.

c. *Learning and work in dynamic tension.* Activity and reflection reinforce each other. Personal growth should be revealed through behavioral change.

d. *Learning that integrates intellectual, emotional, and spiritual dimensions.* Profound growth unites the whole person. It blends body, mind, heart, and soul. Discoveries in one dimension affect all other dimensions.

e. *Learning through laughter and experimentation.* Profound growth cultivates the ability to laugh at oneself, and to risk failure or the appearance of foolishness.

Mission Assumptions
Effective and enduring mission requires:

a. *The timely release of one's spiritual gifts.* Faithful Christians must know and exercise the spiritual gifts with which God created them, and do so courageously when the time seems right.

b. *Maximum confidence to share faith and take risks in service.* Faithful Christians must not only do good deeds, but be able to articulate the religious motivation for those deeds to others. Witness and service must go together.

c. *Authenticity that reveals both vulnerability and strength.*
Faithful Christians must speak and act from the story of
their own life struggle and spiritual victory.
d. *Responsibility for mission by the people who are called to do it.*
Effective mission results only when one moves beyond
supervision and administration, to personally participate
in the work of ministry.
e. *Mutual accountability in a quest for excellence.* Enduring mission results only when the participants work as a team with
others, and demand of themselves the highest standards.

Caring Assumptions
Sensitive care requires:
a. *Mutual support for healing and personal change.* Only constant, planned group support can help individuals overcome destructive addictions to find healing.
b. *The encouragement of healthy intimacy and personal significance.* Honest, respectful sharing should reinforce each
individual's self-worth. The well-being of each participant
should matter to every other participant.
c. *The discovery of meaning through doing.* People find meaning
in life through involvement in activities that have clear,
practical, and significant benefits.
d. *The conviction that those who seek life must give life away.* The
true affirmation of oneself does not come through self-
centeredness, but through self-surrender to a higher purpose.
e. *The confidence that love is a gift to all.* Every person is capable of giving love (not just professional caregivers), and
every person deserves to receive love (not just church
members).

These assumptions lie at the heart of every cell of the Spiritual
Redwood. They are not guarded by a central authority, which must
continually review the performance of each cell to ascertain obedience to principles. There is no need. These assumptions are part
of the genetic code built into the very constitution of every cell. If
the Spiritual Redwood experiences calamity, and only one cell
remains alive, it can replicate the Spiritual Redwood all over again.
Why? Because it carries within itself the imprint of the whole.

Every cell in the Spiritual Redwood provides opportunity and guidance for people to grow. A cell is any group or team in the church. Each group gathers around a leader, and shares a common enthusiasm or affinity. The affinity can be any interest, lifestyle, task, hobby, burden, issue, or concern that passionately bonds people together around a common topic or purpose. Each person who participates in the cell is motivated not only by the shared affinity, but also by a readiness to go deeper into relationships with the others and with God. They are not nominated into the cell, but they are invited to join the cell. Their acceptance of the invitation arises not out of a sense of duty to an institutional agenda, but out of an eagerness to pursue something that they personally believe is supremely important.

> **Cells manifest themselves in small groups.**

Cells rarely exceed twelve persons. They develop their own covenant to gather in whatever ways, in whatever locations, and at whatever times seem best for their group. Whatever the covenant might look like, the cell group members hold one another accountable for their commitments. The structures of each cell may be different, just as their affinities, goals, ideas, and projects will be incredibly diverse. However, each cell demonstrates twin "flows" of relationship building and faith development. These twin "flows" are like an amniotic fluid that swirls and moves within each cell. They are the currents that carry the participants forward eventually to flower into mission.

Within each "flow" there are risks. Spiritual Redwoods train cell leaders to help each cell avoid such perils, and to move the cell forward in the flow. Ultimately, when the time is right, the cell will "multiply" to create two cells. The result is that the Spiritual Redwood grows. These cells may be very small, but their constant multiplication allows the Spiritual Redwood to grow to be the tallest tree in the forest!

Relationship-Building Flow
1. **Conversation** . . . the risk for which is . . . boredom
2. **Information sharing** . . . the risk for which is . . . competition

3. **Ideas and opinions** . . . the risk for which is . . . disagreement
4. **Shared feelings** . . . the risk for which is . . . personality conflict
5. **Dreams and fears** . . . the risk for which is . . . shock
6. **Team vision and action** . . . the risk for which is . . . stagnation
7. **Multiplication** . . . the risk for which is . . . grief.

Conversation begins the relationship flow of the cell. Since participants may be complete strangers, it tends to be introductory and perhaps superficial. The leader helps them to express themselves and feel comfortable, but knows that the cell must move to deeper communication if they are to avoid boredom.

Sharing information is the natural next step in their affinity. They talk about what they love, or, the affinity that has motivated their presence in the first place. People reveal their knowledge, special interests, and questions. The leader helps the cell avoid mere competition, in which individuals begin to try to dominate conversation or position themselves to be "experts" who might "tell" people what to think.

Shared ideas and opinions emerge as the cell builds trust. They risk sharing their perspectives and revealing their ignorance. Conversation becomes more fascinating and even heated. The leader encourages disagreements to emerge, but helps participants find common ground. The greatest challenge is to help the cell accept and respect disagreement that remains unresolved.

Shared feelings will be the next necessary step to deepen relationships. Individuals are encouraged to share their feelings (hurts, joys, tears, laughter) and to recognize irony and mystery. They begin to identify and describe their personalities, perhaps even using a distinct personality inventory. The cell leader helps them understand, accept, and move beyond their personality conflicts.

Sharing deeper dreams and fears brings the cell to a new level of trust and bonding. While the original affinity is still their primary focus of conversation, the cell discovers there is much more to talk about in, through, and beyond this affinity. They begin to understand *why* their affinity is so important to them, and probe *where* their interest or enthusiasm might take them. Prayer becomes more significant. These discoveries may sometimes be shocking times of self-awareness or revelation. The cell leader will try to preserve confidentiality and move the cell to deeper acceptance and mutual support.

Team vision and common action result from the relationship-building process. The combination of enthusiastic affinity, and the new spirit of partnership and unity, leads the cell beyond just talk to action. The cell leader helps them build consensus about an activity which celebrates their unity, and which benefits others beyond the cell.

Multiplication brings the cell to a close, with the positive motivation for participants to move on to other cells or personal disciplines. If the cell remains intact for too long, relationship-building will plateau and personal growth will stagnate. The cell leader helps people address the sadness of "good-bye," by celebrating past cell relationships and future opportunities for growth and service.

Faith-Development Flow
1. **Covenant** . . . the risk for which is . . . indiscipline
2. **Curiosity** . . . the risk for which is . . . consternation
3. **Bible awareness** . . . the risk for which is . . . competition
4. **Trust** . . . the risk for which is . . . dependence
5. **Questioning** . . . the risk for which is . . . fear
6. **Action** . . . the risk for which is . . . judgment
7. **Holy discontent** . . . the risk for which is . . . self-doubt.

Covenant begins the faith-building flow. It builds on the *readiness to go deeper* that is a part of the individual participant's motivation. The covenant may be formal or informal, but it implies a commitment to the group process and the overall environment of spirituality in which the affinity group is based. The leader helps participants understand the importance of commitment.

Curiosity about the spiritual context of the cell is often the initial attitude of participants. They need to know that it is informal, unpressured, not manipulative, and wide open to personal perspective. The cell leader assures the cell that participation does not assume any religious knowledge, or even require any commitments to the church. The only commitment is to the cell itself and to the opportunity for personal depth.

Awareness of the Bible anchors the spirituality of the cell, not denominational polity, tradition, or ideology. In some cells it is simply a process of becoming acquainted with basic scriptural passages to test their relevance to daily living. In other cells it is a more focused process of broadening biblical knowledge. The cell leader helps people move beyond competition over who is "more spiritual" or "more biblically literate," to focus conversation on practical relevance to living.

Trust becomes crucial to the future of the cell. The legitimacy of multiple interpretations and acceptance of disagreement, are combined with recognition of the inner worth of each person and affirmation of the inclusive love of God. The group leader helps people gain confidence in their own quest, and avoid dependence on any one authority for the "right" answers.

Questioning emerges from the deeper trust uncovered by the cell. Participants begin to articulate their doubts and questions, and to dialogue without judgment. They learn to value both clarity and mystery, and understand the meaning of humility. They position themselves for lifelong learning. The cell leader helps them overcome their fears of appearing foolish, making mistakes, or failure.

Action results from the faith-building process. Once again, the cell moves beyond talk to mission. They are motivated by greater clarity about each one's own experience of God, and respect for the diverse experiences of others. Together they want to share the joy of their deeper connection with God beyond the group in some practical way. The cell leader helps them build consensus for a common mission.

Holy discontent brings the cell to a close. Participants become clearer about the individual spiritual paths they need to explore, and become restless to move forward. If the cell stays together too long, their faith-building will plateau, and their spirituality will stagnate. The cell leader helps people find the self-confidence to move forward in their personal faith journeys.

The cells of the Spiritual Redwood are in constant process. Not only are the participants within each cell growing and changing, but the cells themselves evolve and multiply. Each cell is time-limited. The time limit will vary from cell to cell, but eventually the process of cellular growth brings the small group to an inevitable end. However, the cell does not die; it multiplies! A new group gathers around the emerging nucleus of another leader, and eventually the cell splits into two. The newly formed cells may share the same affinity, but such redundancy is a matter of celebration rather than alarm. On the other hand, the newly formed cells may develop around completely different affinities, structure themselves in completely different ways, and covenant together for very different purposes.

Some cells may be oriented primarily around *discovery*. The primary orientation of the cell is to grow in self-awareness, respect for others, and faith in God. Participants discern their spiritual gifts, learn how to relate to others in deep and trusting intimacy, and deepen their relationship with Jesus. Along the way, they may experience healing, gain knowledge, build insight, broaden perspective, or focus priorities.

Some cells may be oriented primarily around *destiny*. The primary orientation of the cell is to listen for the callings of God and discern how one's gifts can be used effectively to pass life on to others. Participants develop disciplines of prayer and meditation, Bible study and spiritual reflection, all of which lead them to the very practical discovery of the ministry or mission to which God beckons them. Such ministries or missions simultaneously bring life-giving benefits to others and joyous self-fulfillment.

The experience of cellular life never ends, because growth never stops. All activities in the Spiritual Redwood are relational, dynamic, and purposeful. Every participant is committed to growth, and growth can only occur through quality relationships. Every cell is committed to growth, and growth can only occur through planned flows of relationship-building and faith-building. The Spiritual Redwood is committed to growth, and growth can only happen when every unit, from the greatest branch to the tiniest tendril, is passionate about growth.

Team Ministries

Participants in the Spiritual Redwood do not act alone. They live in relationships, and they work in teams. The "flows" within cellular life always bring people to ministry. Life is never contained within the cell, but it overflows the cell to bring life to the forest. The fullness of Christian identity is revealed only in loving relationships, and the fullness of Christian maturity is revealed only in practical ministries.

Spiritual Redwoods thrive on relationships.

The "Ministry Team" is another form of cell life in the Spiritual Redwood. The affinities that bind the team together are always an explicitly stated mission, and the motivations for team membership are always intensely felt spiritual calls. These missions may be very imaginative or quite practical, very simple or incredibly complex. Common forms of Ministry Teams include:

> Worship teams
> Teaching teams
> Small group leaders
> Care and counseling teams
> Visitation teams
> Advocacy teams
> Administration teams
> Prayer teams
> Visioning teams
> Salaried pastoral teams
> Mission teams

Whatever the activity might be, large or small, the members of the team engage in it with a zeal for excellence, because they understand the activity to be a vehicle through which abundant life can be shared with others.

Ministry teams are oriented around a predetermined, clearly defined mission chosen by the team leader. Teams exist to accomplish ministry, not simply to debate or manage ministry. They share a passion for the work. Even strategic planning teams are given a specific charge prior to forming. They do not meet merely to discuss the future of the church. They meet to develop a plan that solves a particular problem or accomplishes a particular goal.

Ministry teams are chosen by the team leader. Team members are not thrown together by a church board, nor are team members selected because they represent various special interest groups. They are handpicked by the team leader on the basis of their commitment, sense of urgency, unique technical skills, and readiness to cooperate with the team. They represent no one but themselves. Their energies are devoted entirely to getting the mission accomplished, not with reporting to a constituency.

Ministry teams are formed with people who have trained

skills. Teams are no more effective than the individuals who form the team. Skilled people form skilled teams. Therefore, Spiritual Redwoods train potential team members before they even join the team, and then provide regular opportunities for teams to upgrade their skills.

Ministry teams harmonize competency and passion. The best teams integrate the gifts, skills, enthusiasms, and dreams of each team member. Individual members of the team not only do what they do best, but they do what they love the most. Together the team shares commitment to the vision, values, beliefs, and mission that is the essence of the Spiritual Redwood; a sense of urgency for the mission to be accomplished; and technical skills in each member's particular area.

Ministry teams are formed with people who enjoy cooperation. Although team members all share entrepreneurial ability, there are no "Lone Rangers" in an effective team. Each team member respects the power of the other members of the team to enhance one another's expertise for the common good. All share the credit, and all share the blame.

Ministry teams value all work equally. Team members exercise their spiritual gifts, whatever they may be, and no gift is superior to any other gift. The people in the "background" of a mission are no less important than the people in the "forefront" of the mission. The people who do the smallest, practical tasks, have equal significance for the mission and equal voice in the team.

Ministry teams exercise power for the common good. Ministry teams can design and implement mission on their own authority. Their power is always exercised, however, within the vision, values, beliefs, and mission that are essential to the Spiritual Redwood. The interaction of team members with one another, and Ministry Teams with other teams, is guided by the Golden Rule.

Ministry teams communicate constantly. Team members are in continuous conversation as they do the work of the team. They freely interrupt one another, test ideas with one another, and time their work to speed the work of each member. Whenever the common good demands it, or whenever potential opportunities emerge, the team communicates directly with any other cell or leader in the Spiritual Redwood. Middle management is kept to a minimum.

Lay Pastors

Already we have spoken of the importance of leadership for each cell or ministry team. These "Lay Pastors" are the nuclei around which each cell forms. They are the basic caregivers of the twenty-first-century congregation. The transition from congregations dependent on clergy for pastoral care and leadership, to congregations that rely on gifted, called, and equipped laity for pastoral care and leadership, is the greater paradigm shift that lies behind the growth of cell groups.

> Lay Pastors are to the Spiritual Redwood what ministers were to the churches of Christendom.

Any group that meets at least once a month will have a Lay Pastor. Three basic types of Lay Pastors are emerging in the Spiritual Redwood, although the potential variations in leadership are infinite:

1. Small group leaders who guide people in *discovery* and discernment of *destiny*
2. Ministry team leaders who lead specific missions (e.g., visitations, prison ministries, food banks, music, etc.) or who lead regular activities (e.g., greeters, parking attendants, book sales, etc.)
3. Administration team leaders who manage finance, property, or personnel.

Lay Pastors are the primary caregivers of the Spiritual Redwood and the effective "pastors" to the people of their group or team. They are all engaged in nurturing, equipping, or deploying ministries within the Spiritual Redwood, and beyond in the cultural forest.

Bill first became aware of how widespread this transition has become when he visited a Spiritual Redwood in Houston, Texas. Entering the church building, he immediately noticed the many pictures of individuals and couples surrounding the lobby. Who were they? "They are the Lay Pastors of the church," came the reply. Fifty to sixty pictures filled the walls. Why were these faces so prominently displayed? "Because we want more Lay Pastors, we praise the ones that we have!" Quite different from the custom of many churches to line a wall with the pictures of past "senior pastors."

It has always been our experience as pastors that laypeople often carry out a ministry better than the clergy. They give more time, offer more sensitivity, and establish more credibility than a paid professional. The research of Lyle Schaller reveals that newcomers are 75 percent more likely to return when visited first by a layperson. We've known laypeople to spend hours in the hospital caring for a parishioner, while the clergy dash off to another bedside.

Since the cultural forest has changed, with the jungle of human need encroaching upon every side, a new kind of credible Christian is emerging. In the twentieth century, the "Credible Christian" was defined by the experience and needs of a society that was identifiably "Christian." The public all had a basic understanding of Scripture and doctrine, and were all generally sympathetic to the institutional church. The "Credible Christian" was:

- A *clergyperson* with denominational and academic credentials . . .
- Who was *oriented* around the *polity and doctrine of a church institution* . . .
- Who had been *trained to manage ecclesiastical work* and *take care of people* . . .
- Who had been *equipped with liturgical skills* and *historical perspectives* . . .
- Who was *professionally authoritative* and *knowledgeable of "eternal truths"* . . .
- And who was *supported by a denominational association.*

As we begin the twenty-first century, however, this society has disappeared. Today society is no longer identifiably "Christian." The public do not have even the most basic understanding of Scripture or doctrine. They are not only unsympathetic with the institutional church but generally hostile to it. The credibility of the leadership just described is sinking fast.

In the twenty-first century, the "Credible Christian" is now defined by the experience and needs of a public that is profoundly spiritually yearning, and yet deeply alienated from the institutional church. The emerging "Credible Christian" for the twenty-first century is:

- A *layperson* with personal authenticity and spiritual integrity . . .
- Who has *answered* for herself or himself *the Key Question:*

What is it about my experience of Jesus that this community cannot live without? . . .

- Who exercises *spiritual gifts from God* to *relate in healthy ways* to others . . .
- Who has been *equipped* by the church with *interpersonal skills and biblical insight* . . .
- Who is personally *humble and on a high learning curve* . . .
- And who is *supported by trusted, intimate colleagues.*

These Christians become the Lay Pastors of the Spiritual Redwood. Individuals may be invited to be Lay Pastors because they exhibit a passion for a particular ministry, or because they have been identified through a "Spiritual Gifts Inventory," or simply because they celebrate a call. In all cases, laity are encouraged to discover what God wants them to do with their life.

> The credible Christian is no longer a professional "clergyperson."

Bill wrote about the Christ United Methodist Church (Fort Lauderdale, Florida) model in *Sacred Cows Make Gourmet Burgers*. It is a good example of the permission-giving organization and Lay Pastor leadership of the Spiritual Redwood. In this example, any layperson can celebrate a calling to some form of ministry, and, provided that it is within the three core values of the church, take initiative for it without needing to ask permission. They are not recruited by the church, but they emerge from the movement of the Holy Spirit. There are only four simple criteria for being a Lay Pastor.

1. *Commitment to daily prayer and Scripture reading.* After all, no one can share what they do not have. This daily discipline feeds the Lay Pastor, enables them to focus their ministries, and guides them to pray for the people within their care.

2. *Commitment to prayer for their ministry.* Whatever the affinity of the cell group or the activity of the Ministry Team, the leader gathers the group for prayer and deep sharing. Personal concerns and celebrations from the previous week are noted, and participants pray for one another.

3. *Commitment to monthly training.* Lay Pastors must attend a one-hour training session every month. Spouses and friends are welcome to attend. All Lay Pastors must be present. Here they are trained, equipped, and encouraged to lead their ministry area by the pastor of Christ Church. They focus on what God is doing in the lives of people, and help one another address emerging obstacles or issues.

4. *Commitment to individual coaching.* Every Lay Pastor updates the staff each month regarding their ministry. The staff know who has been added to the ministry or who is being missed. Key obstacles or opportunities are identified, and the staff can offer twenty-four-hour coaching and support.

In this example from Christ Church, the former distinctions of Christendom between "clergy" and "laity" are erased.

It is vital to understand that the group leader is *not* merely a facilitator, nor is this leader necessarily an "expert" in biblical interpretation, liturgy and worship, psychotherapy, or group process. The group leader is simply the effective "Pastor" or "Shepherd" of the group. The Lay Pastor is to the pre-Christian Spiritual Redwood, what the Minister was to the churches of Christendom.

Their leadership affects the lives of participants beyond the group meeting. They are available to "coach" and "support" individual participants throughout the week and may be the first persons contacted by a group participant in the event of personal crisis. The group leader may even become the key worship leader for funerals, weddings, and other special occasions for group participants. The authenticity of their faith, the depth of their compassion, and the clarity of their vision helps people find their way through the ambiguities of daily life.

> All people are gifted, and all Christians are called.

No specific personality type is required for group leadership. However, Lay Pastors will *know* their personality type and use that knowledge to interact with group participants effectively. The primary issue in recognizing Lay Pastors is not personality, but integrity and style.

Lay Pastor Integrity

Deep, daily spirituality—Has clearly focused faith that pervades both personal and professional life

Intentional confidentiality—Invites immediate trust, gives reliable guarantees to preserve secrets

Unswerving fidelity—Exhibits loyalty in personal relationships, no hint of sexual exploitation, or flirtatious and abusive behavior

Commitment to equality—Avoids stereotypes of race, sex, generation, lifestyle; encourages respect, treats others with fairness

Personal humility—Is always eager to learn and grow; does not fear ambiguity or paradox

Self-directed, self-disciplined—Works hard, toward clear goals, with internalized motivation for excellence.

In the twenty-first century, the public looks for authentic "mentors" who can support and guide them through the ambiguities of life. Such mentors may not be learned, but they are regarded as wise. They may not be articulate orators, but they are effective one-to-one communicators. They are absolutely trustworthy; their company is safe and reliable; they take care to respect others. They never rely on authorities to direct their course, but possess an inner compass that directs their living.

> Lay Pastors are:
> coaches
> mentors
> guides
> midwives
> transformers.

Lay Pastor Style

Habitual patience—Waits and prays for the work of the Holy Spirit; does not rush people or prematurely resolve differences

Broad vision—Locates experiences in a broader context of culture and history; discerns experience in a broader flow of purpose; celebrates diversity of lifestyle and opinion

Gentleness—Is kind, sympathetic; recognizes and assists others to overcome obstacles

Courageous perception—Sees the point, faces contradiction, identifies the crux of decision making

People focus—Prioritizes persons above issues, dialogue above agendas, growth above success

Inclusive behavior—Is sensitive to silence, invites people to participate, is alert to the fringes of groups.

In the twenty-first century, the public looks for spiritual "midwives" who can help them birth their dreams and hopes. Such midwives may not be accredited professionals or officeholders, but they are regarded as transformers. They may not be managers or administrators, but they are effective motivators for personal growth. They wait for truth to emerge from within, without imposing truth from beyond. They simultaneously nurture and challenge the individual.

Staff Support

Since missions and ministries are accomplished by the cells (Small Group and Ministry Teams) of the Spiritual Redwood, guided by Lay Pastors, the salaried staff have an important role to play. They may not *do* the ministry, but they must help motivate, equip, and coach the cells and cell leaders. They must have the skills to move among multiple teams during the year—even at the same time.

Paid staff do not do ministry.

For example, the emerging mission may be to start a new worship service during the week. This will require a team composed of persons skilled in worship, music, discipling, and outreach . . . plus others skilled in technology support, prayer support . . . plus still others skilled in organizational support for refreshments, parking, and resource displays. Some of these team members may already be involved in other teams related to each topic.

Quality staff support assumes that staff share commitment to the overall vision, values, beliefs, and mission that form the essence of the Spiritual Redwood. They need to have a clear sense of personal identity and direction in life, good social skills, a passionate sense of urgency, and a variety of strong technical skills. They will need to display courage, decisiveness, imagination, and integrity. Most important, they will need to be comfortable with playing a variety of roles in each team, without ignoring the larger picture of mission beyond any given team.

Trust is essential. The Ministry Teams must have autonomous power to design, implement, and evaluate their mission activities without requiring approvals from the staff. The staff are there to motivate, equip, and coach, and will help integrate the mission of the cell into the larger mission of the Spiritual Redwood, but they are not there to give or deny permission for action. Since this represents a dramatic change from the traditional roles of "clergy" in the church, it is understandable that staff may find this change stressful.

Trust can be developed in churches transforming to become Spiritual Redwoods, in six stages.

1. Commitment to the idea of cell groups doing ministries. Every staff person must be enthusiastic about this strategy of mission. They must be committed to becoming a Spiritual Redwood. They must be ready to relinquish control. This first stage does not involve the acquisition of a new skill, but the changing of an attitude. If a staff member cannot change this attitude through coaching, counseling, and prayer, then it is likely that the staff member will not have a place with the salaried leadership of the Spiritual Redwood.

THE RISK-LEARN CYCLE

Figure 6.2

2. **Understanding of the role of staff as motivators, equippers, and coaches.** Every staff person must be trained for the new roles. "Expository Preachers," for example, will likely need to be retrained in motivational and conversational speaking. Information and skills that were kept to oneself in order to safeguard power, now need to be shared openly to share power. Professionals who managed time by separating personal and career time, now need to learn to manage time as they offer twenty-four-hour coaching support. Often there are laypersons who can assist the clergy in learning these new skills. For example, a "Toastmaster" coached a preacher in motivational speaking, a public-school teacher helped another staff member learn group process, and an emergency room nurse assisted still other staff to understand the nature of "coaching."

3. **Readiness to embrace chaos, as one would embrace an old friend.** In addition to an attitude that affirms the way ministry gets done in a Spiritual Redwood, and acquired skills to motivate, equip, and coach others, staff members must be able to live calmly in the midst of confusion. They need to be able to live comfortably and confidently, not just in the midst of change, but in the midst of *constant* change. They will need to learn new conflict resolution skills, and practice the "Risk-Learn Cycle" (figure 6.2).

Staff learn to risk, experience failure, learn from mistakes, redesign mission, and try again. Those who are uncomfortable with periodically looking foolish, or who are unable to ask for help, will have difficulty serving a Spiritual Redwood.

4. **Participation in disciplines that foster trust.** It is possible to design structures of communication and mutual support that will build confidence between staff and Lay Pastors. Weekly fax and electronic mail can speed communication and consultation. Periodic retreats, weekly small groups, the staff's setting the meeting agenda, prayer teams, and fellowship meals all help build deeper trust. However, staff must be committed to prioritizing time for this structure.

5. **Small group support.** Staff meetings must function like cell groups. That is, they must include prayer, intimate sharing, and biblical reflection, in addition to the agenda of planning and action. Large staffs can meet in smaller units. Staff can share personal dreams and fears, profound doubts and new insights, in an environment in which each person can offer pastoral support to another. Clergy and support staff are equal.

6. Shared affinity. The final step to building trust is the discovery that you respect and like one another. It only takes one irreconcilable conflict or irresponsible behavior pattern to destroy group trust that has taken time and effort to create. Diversity in personality, spiritual gifts, skills, and perspectives can all be welcome within an environment of genuine affection.

Once the staff have achieved this context of trust among themselves, they can nurture that trust throughout the entire life of the Spiritual Redwood. Trust is in the very air that the Spiritual Redwood breathes. Spiritual Redwoods must have confidence in their Lay Pastors. They must know that their Lay Pastors . . .

- are gifted in their ministries
- are called to their ministries
- are equipped to do their ministries with skill
- are committed to upgrading their skills in a plan for quality.

The staff will help the Lay Pastors discern their gifts and callings, equip them with everything they need to pursue those callings, and regularly support them to do better, grow deeper, and reach farther.

The Spiritual Redwood is not a structure composed of enduring committees, requiring the coordination of an extensive middle management. It is a "self-starting" organism that nurtures initiative. Within the boundaries of core vision, beliefs, and values, there is a veritable chaos of cells that are growing, changing, combining, dying, and multiplying. There is a macrocosm, and there are innumerable microcosms, but there is no need for bureaucracy or middle management.

The Spiritual Redwood is fluid and flexible, rather than rigid and predictable. It is not a structure, but a movement. It is not a hierarchy of control, but a web of shared values. It is the minimum corporate identity necessary to foster the most spiritual entrepreneurship possible. The chaos is not held together by a central ordained authority, a bureaucratic process, a propositional agreement around ideology or theology, or a denominational polity. Indeed, the chaos within a Spiritual Redwood will shatter all these weak attempts to contain its creative power. Only four things guide and harmonize the chaos:

1. The energy field of core vision, beliefs, values, and mission that is the very "essence of the species" imprinted in every cell
2. The strands of faith, learning, mission, and caring assumptions which are part of the genetic code built directly into every cell
3. The amniotic fluid of simultaneous relationship-building and faith-building, which is the flow of activity within every cell
4. The leadership that forms the nucleus of every cell . . . that is gifted, called, and equipped . . . and that shares a common quest for quality.

These four factors nurture each cell to maintain the balance between *Freedom* and *Covenant* that is the organizational core of the species.

Governance is held to a minimum. The accountability of the organization is summarized in just four key questions:

1. Is there any way in which a cell has gone beyond the boundaries of core vision, beliefs, values, and mission, so that the cell no longer reflects the imprint of the essence of the species?
2. Have the strands of theological, educational, mission, and pastoral assumptions been broken in the life of the cell?
3. Has the flow of relationship-building and faith-building within the cell plateaued or stagnated at any stage?
4. Has the leadership of the cell failed in any way to pursue a common quest for quality?

These are the questions every cell continually asks within its own life, and that Lay Pastors and staff ask of each other as they regularly meet together. If the answer is yes to any of these questions, then together they will solve the problem. If the answer is no, then no matter how creative, fantastic, imaginative, or challenging the ministry might be, they are free to pursue it.

Spiritual Giants

In the midst of every Spiritual Redwood, there is a Spiritual Giant. Groups and Ministry Teams do not replace the need for an entrepreneurial individual at the center of the organization. In the book *The Paradox Principle,* the Price Waterhouse team reports their study of several successful, prominent organizations. They found that every organization with an effective team-based work process has an extremely strong leader at the center of the organization.[2] Our experience with congregations all across North America verifies this insight. Dynamic ministries that use Ministry Teams and Small Groups all require strong leadership at the center of the chaos.

This leader is not a controller, who gives or withholds permission. This leader is not an authoritarian, who relies on denominational certifications or entitlements to always have the last word. This leader is not a dictator, who tells people where to go or what to do. This leader is not a judge, who decides whether people are saved or lost. This leader is not "The Minister," who takes care of all the people and does all the ministry.

This individual is always a *visionary.* The leader of the organization has the ability to listen to and perceive the hidden yearnings of the public. The leader has the intense imagination to invent new and practical ways for the gospel to address needs, invite participation, nurture leadership, and release mission.

This individual is always a *synthesizer.* The leader of the organization has the ability to bring together seemingly contradictory ideas, incompatible personalities, and paradoxical trends, and create a synergy of effort that is surprisingly effective and profound.

This individual is always a *motivator.* The leader of the organization has the ability to inspire vision and action in others. The leader has the ability to hearten and encourage others, build self-esteem and excitement, and multiply joy and enthusiasm for the entire organization.

Such a leader is sometimes called "The Pastor," but such Christendom terminology does not truly describe the role of this leader. This leader does lead the staff, and this leader does nurture the Lay Pastors. The most profound impact of this leadership, however, is that such leaders help others give birth to the gifts, callings, and leadership that lie within them. It is to the description of this new leadership for the pre-Christian era that we now turn.

Every great team has a great leader.

_____

2. Price Waterhouse Change Integration Team, *The Paradox Principle* (Chicago: Irwin Publishers, 1996).

VISTA SEVEN

Birthing the Fruits of Life

Leadership

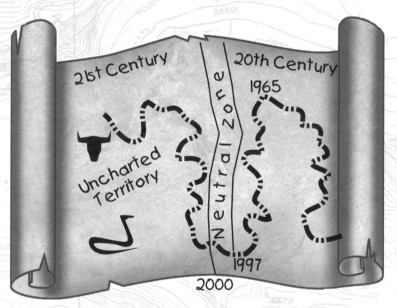

Spiritual midwives are required along the journey to the twenty-first century.

*T*he journey through the forest inspires a new respect for mystery. Things happen that are unpredictable. Organisms grow in ways that don't make sense. That is to say, the forest continually defeats the categories and expectations civilized pioneers seek to impose upon it. Those who would live in the forest must learn the ways of the forest, and not expect the forest to rearrange itself for the sake of civilization. They must know the forest, but not as a researcher "knows" the data, and not as an institution "knows" the market. They must "befriend" the forest. Their "knowing" must be person-to-person and face-to-face.

In the folklore of all peoples, trees have been endowed with personhood. They have been given names and treated with a respect normally reserved for the elders of the village. Oak trees among the Celts, pine trees among the Romans, and grapevines among the Greeks have all been personified in various ways. The Redwood itself has been treated as an equal partner in life by many native peoples. Folklore from Appalachia motivated artisans to carve faces from the bark of trees, hinting that within that whole diversity of leaves, branches, and roots, there was a person.

It is significant that nowhere do ordinary folk ever conceive "the person within the tree" to be a committee. The person is always an individual. This individual is greeted as a friend. This friend shares mutually beneficial partnerships. The "person within the tree" is a catalyst for positive change. The "person within the tree" does not dominate, control, or manage the diverse life within the tree, or beyond in the forest, in the manner civilization might expect. Instead, this "person within the tree" articulates a vision, or personifies an identity, that synthesizes diversity and inspires individual fulfillment.

One cannot dominate this forest. One can only forge partnerships for growth. Inability to form partnerships which can give birth to new life brings inevitable death. The Redwood may be described as one great, dynamic "synergy" of life. It is the combined or cooperative action of multiple cells that together increase one another's effectiveness. It is a whole that is greater than the sum of all its parts, because as a dynamic unity it gives birth to new life.

In order to understand the unfolding revolution in church leadership that is incorporated into Spiritual Redwoods, it is crucial to understand the new reality of spiritual yearning "within the forest" of contemporary culture.

Christians from the age of Constantine onward increasingly relied upon *mediated experiences* of God. They made meaningful

> **We are experiencing a revolution in our understanding of leadership.**

connections with God through authoritative persons and offices; liturgies and rites; icons, symbols, and architectures; organizations, denominations, and institutions. Protestantism modified the nature of the mediation, but not the need for mediation. Certified and authoritative clergy still explained eternal truths, while liturgies and ritual practices still assisted Christians to make connections with God. Mediation helped them understand how to build their lives in the imitation of Christ.

Of course, the mediated experiences of God during the age of Christendom were not shallow, and the Christians who depended on them were not shallow Christians. Denominations diligently sought to certify clergy with greater care, create ever more profound and relevant liturgies, and develop ever more contemporary architectures and symbols—all intended to deepen the mediated experience of God. In the twentieth century, intentionality about entitlements reached its zenith, and liturgical renewal reached new heights—while at the same time participation in institutional churches dropped dramatically.

What happened? Christendom came to an end—and a pre-Christian era began.

What distinguishes the spiritually seeking public of the pre-Christian age, from the experience of Christians during the age of Christendom, is the high priority they place on *the immediate experience of God.* Mediated experiences of God, no matter how carefully deployed and planned, are no longer sufficient for the new spiritual hunger today. The mere presence of God means nothing; the touch of the Holy means everything.

> **People need to experience God, not be told about God.**

Pre-Christian seekers do not want to imitate Christ. They want to touch the hem of his robe, listen to his mentoring words, and walk daily with the risen Lord. They know that Jesus understands them, because he is the *"man of sorrows."*

Of course, seekers of the pre-Christian twenty-first century are not any better or deeper than church people of the age of

Christendom—they are just different. They seek direct connections with God. These direct connections may be established through passive meditation or active social service, through private self-discovery or intimate sharing and corporate celebration. However the connection is made, the immediate experience of God authenticates religious experience by making it highly individual, spontaneous, and creative.

The Mediated Experience of God

Figure 7.1

What distinguishes the spiritually seeking public of the pre-Christian age is the high priority they place on *the uncontrollable experience of the Holy*. Mediated experiences of God are essentially *controlled* experiences of the Holy. Church leaders and church institutions were "controllers," guarding and guiding access to religious experience. It was as if an enormous, mysterious ocean of divinity lay just over the horizon. Church leaders and institutions created aqueducts and channels, which tapped the waters in measured amounts, selecting the destinations of grace in measured amounts ... lest a tidal wave of water sweep people away, or lest unwary spiritual "amateurs" should plunge directly into the ocean and drown. The role of church leadership was to create the conduits of meaning

The Immediate Experience of God

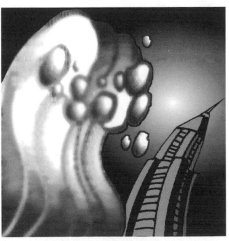

Figure 7.2

through which the power of God might not only flow, but be rendered intelligible.

The immediate experience of God implies *uncontrollable experiences of the Holy*. Such experiences overflow the institutional conduits created by past church leadership. They carry the grace of God in unexpected directions and in unmeasured amounts. They overflow the boundaries of rationality and intelligibility. They replace mere understanding with indescribable joy and awe. They lead the spiritual seeker beyond prose and liturgy, to poetry, song, and dance. In the pre-Christian "forest," there are no distinctions between spiritual "amateurs" and "experts," but all alike may be carried away by tidal waves or leap into spiritual depths.

Spiritual Redwoods grow in a culture in which surprise and shock are everyday experiences. The unusual, the odd, the abnormal, and the bizarre are commonplace. Beneath the surface of rationality, there is a turbulent, churning, seething mystery about life. This dimension of depth is simultaneously welcomed and feared. The irrational blends into the rational. Who could ever have imagined that a virus could survive the combined efforts of modern medicine seeking a cure, and prey upon the one thing most valued by modern people: human intimacy? And who could ever have imagined that *in vitro* fertilization could ever become a simple, standardized medical procedure that could bring unanticipated joy to women and men who thought they would never experience birth?

Spiritual Redwoods require leaders who are spiritual giants. These are not leaders in the traditional ways of Christendom. They do not control the work, manage the work, or even do the work of the church. They are visionaries, synthesizers, and motivators. They move within a cultural forest in which the collision between rationality and irrationality leads to constant surprises. If the Spiritual Redwood is a synergy of life, then leaders who are spiritual giants must be "synergists" who build synergies for life.

Throughout history, God has worked through spiritual giants who could envision radically new futures, synthesize extraordinarily different cultures and ideas, and motivate people to energetically become all that God wanted them to be. These have been people like:

- Miriam, Moses, Deborah, and Ruth
- Lydia, Priscilla, Paul, and Timothy

- Augustine, Perpetua, Benedict, and Patrick
- Martin Luther, John of the Cross, Clare of Assisi, John Wesley
- Martin Luther King, Jr., Rosa Parks, Mother Teresa, Nelson Mandela.

These are ordinary individuals. Yet God transforms the ordinary into the extraordinary, for the sole purpose of encouraging others to attempt the impossible for God. In a culture of seemingly insurmountable obstacles, shocking evils, and unexpected dangers, the very notion of giving birth to new life seems to be an impossible dream. Spiritual giants help people do it.

Not long ago a leadership seminar gathered pastors from many denominations and backgrounds. We shared with the group the visions, strategies, and principles emerging for the church in the pre-Christian, twenty-first century. During the evaluation at the end of the event, we asked them how they felt. One person spoke for many, saying, "*I feel threatened as all get out!*" Why are church leaders (whether they are called "clergy" or "laity") feeling so threatened?

First, church leaders are called to LEAD! The cultural forest is encroaching on the institutional church on every side. The distinctions between the "sacred" and the "secular" have disappeared. The Christian faith is being increasingly obscured by wild speculations on the one hand and entrenched traditionalism on the other. The general public feels lost, and the Christian public feel powerless. In the midst of such challenge, church leaders are extraordinarily timid. They are terrified that they might be perceived to be too aggressive, too disruptive, or too dictatorial. They cling to the myth that the *less leadership* they offer, the *more empowered* Christians will be! In fact, the opposite is true. We remind our colleagues of the findings of the 1996 Price Waterhouse team: "*Where leadership is clearly in evidence, the benefits of empowerment are being achieved and embedded in the culture.*"[1] Church leaders are called to risk popularity, social status, and pension plans, in order to empower others to envision, birth, and nurture the God-given potential that is within them.

---

1. Price Waterhouse Change Integration Team, *The Paradox Principle* (Chicago: Irwin Publishers, 1996), p. 142.

**Second, church leaders are called to lead WITH DIFFER-
ENT SKILLS!** Many of the skills that clergy leaders learned from
seminary, or that layleaders learned from years of institutional
church experience, are irrelevant for the pre-Christian world.
Expository preaching, lectionary-based liturgies, classical and traditional music, large group administration, institutional management, and many other skills are becoming useless among a society
of alienated seekers. The top two weaknesses church leaders share
with us in workshops across North America are *"We don't know how
to pray"* and *"We don't know how to share our faith."* Spiritual leaders
in the new era require skills in faith-sharing, designing spiritual
disciplines, mentoring, nurturing small groups, designing and
leading indigenous worship, conflict resolution, and living effectively in the midst of chaos.

**Third, church leaders are called to BE AUTHENTICAL-
LY SPIRITUAL PEOPLE!** The old credentialing processes that
certified leaders of the church are no longer credible or convinc-
ing. No one cares whether or not the clergy are entitled to use the

TWENTY-FIRST-CENTURY LEADERSHIP ASSUMPTIONS

- Leadership is needed today more than at any other time in history.

- People yearn to be led.

- All revival comes from strong leaders.

- Without effective leaders people do not grow.

- Effective teams always have at least one strong leader.

- Leadership is an event involving more than one person.

word "Reverend," wear preaching stoles, or place abbreviations for "Masters" or "Doctoral" degrees after their name. No one cares whether or not layleaders have served many years in church management, or have been elected to be lifetime "Elders" or "Deacons" in the church institution, or have served higher offices in diocese, presbytery, or conference. What matters is that leaders truly live their faith and can readily and joyfully speak out of their own life struggles and spiritual victories.

Spirituality is more important than credentials.

Over and over again, we have asserted that the world, and the church world, have dramatically changed at the end of the twentieth century. We live at a time of "paradigm shifts," "earthquakes," and "cracks in history." Leadership cannot be the same for the twenty-first century. Here are some of the reasons most church leaders are finding it harder and harder to give effective leadership:

Revolutionary change: For centuries, change has been slow and evolutionary. Leaders could easily draw on lessons learned from the past, slowly introduce change to lower stress, and continue business as usual. Now change is revolutionary, rapid, and absolutely urgent.

Essential relationships: Since the Enlightenment, society has prized autonomous individuality. The industrial economy treated people as separate units. Leaders could work one-to-one, and create realms of influence that were protected and unassailable. Now rapid sharing of information and teamwork is crucial within, and between, all organizations.

Multiple cultures: For centuries, immigration to North America has been slow, individual, and primarily European. Leaders could assume a fundamental homogeneity of race and culture, and assimilate one individual at a time into the church.

	Now immigration is rapid, collective, and global. Radical diversity typifies every neighborhood, and displaced peoples are finding their place in the community.
Zero starting points:	For decades, mainstream denominations were preeminent in North America, and most people were raised in institutional churches. Leaders could assume that newcomers already had some foundation in Christian faith. Now the public have little Christian foundation, and churches can assume nothing.
Motivational curiosity:	For years, pragmatic North American churches assumed that *"actions would speak louder than words."* They did good deeds assuming that everyone would recognize the faith that lay behind them. Today even the best deeds are received with suspicion. People are alert to "hidden agendas" and secretly manipulative purposes. They distrust empty altruism. They want to know one's motivation. They want to hear the concrete faith that lies behind our actions.
Church shopping:	Denominational loyalty, which peaked in the first half of the twentieth century, has rapidly waned. Leaders once could rely on traditional practices and policies to meet the needs of people. Now denominational loyalty no longer exists. Leaders either meet the changing needs and yearnings of people, or the people go somewhere else.
Mobile Christians:	Until the 1960s, neighborhoods determined where people would worship. Leaders assumed people would attend the denominational church closest to

their residence. If they drove, each car would bring at least four persons. Now, Christians drive miles to whatever community of faith will meet their needs— and each car brings only one or two persons, with some families arriving in more than one car.

Equipped disciples: During the first two-thirds of the twentieth century, most church people assumed that professional salaried clergy did ministry. Highly respected in the community, they were hired as personal chaplains to a congregation. Now professional congregational chaplains have little respect, and younger generations demand quality support that enables them to do the ministry.

Indigenous worship: During most of the twentieth century, worship consisted of a few songs, printed liturgies, and a sermon, loosely organized around the Christian year. Leaders could rely on the organ, quote from books, and explore the lectionary. Now, music is the dominant form of communication, technologies are visual and experiential, faith-sharing is essential, and the three most significant holidays are Christmas, Thanksgiving, and Halloween.

This is not an exhaustive list of reasons why church leaders are finding it harder and harder to give effective leadership, but it identifies many of the key cultural revolutions that are rendering old leadership styles and methods obsolete. The challenge of the biblical story is clear. If today's church leaders cannot adopt new styles and methods, and define for themselves a whole new

> Leaders who work harder, longer, and smarter in the same old way kill the church even faster.

identity and purpose, then God will raise up spiritual giants elsewhere.

The leadership dilemma of Christendom at the close of the twentieth century is that it is trapped between a polarization of "dictators" and "enablers."

"Dictators"	. . . tell people what to do, control how they do it, and evaluate the results using ecclesiastical criteria.
"Dictators"	lead people to a goal whether or not they want to go there. They leverage people into action through authoritarian command or manipulative guilt.
"Enablers"	. . . ask people what they want to do, help them do whatever they want to do, and evaluate the results by counting the number of people involved.
"Enablers"	lead people to any goal of their choosing. They leverage people into action through correct information or manipulative management.

In either case, leadership training usually begins by listing various "characteristics" of good leadership. "Dictators" need a powerful charisma, expertise in doctrine and denominational polity, supremely articulate corporate communication skills, absolute clarity about the truth, and thick skins. "Enablers" need a nonaggressive personality, expertise in psychology and group process, supremely articulate one-to-one communication skills, deliberate lack of clarity about the truth, and thin skins. Both need to possess skills in liturgical worship, institutional management, and conflict resolution. "Dictators" build organizational machines that are either hierarchical or dysfunctional. "Enablers" build organizational machines that are either *benevolently* hierarchical or dysfunctional.

The Leadership Event	
Twentieth Century	*Twenty-First Century*
Hierarchy	Initiative
Bureaucracy	Teams
Leader and followers	Leaders and allies
Power to cause change	Influence to shape processes
Authority over people	Authenticity in relationships
Self-assurance	Trust in others
Deductive analysis	Inductive synthesis
Excellence in performance	Sincerity of purpose
Quantified outcomes	Quality processes

Spiritual Redwoods come to the understanding of leadership in a different way. They perceive that leadership is not a list of characteristics, but an *event* involving more than one person that motivates individuals passionately to pursue a direction. In order to understand leadership in the Spiritual Redwood, we do not first list characteristics. We identify the key metaphor for action.

The "Midwife" Metaphor

Fundamentally, Spiritual Redwood leadership is best understood through metaphor, rather than through analysis. No specific set of personality traits or professional skills can adequately describe the leaders of Spiritual Redwoods. They "break the molds" of Christendom. The terminology that will adequately define them has yet to be invented. They are a different species of leader. As we searched for a metaphor, we knew only that the metaphor must describe a person who is:

Midwife, the key metaphor

A Visionary . . . who is convinced of a truth beyond self, and readily embraces a mysterious future that cannot be fully understood or controlled.

A Synthesizer	. . . who can build a shared vision that integrates complexity, and brings opposites into a creative new unity.
A Motivator	. . . who can communicate excitement as well as knowledge, and empower people to fulfill their dreams by doing what they most fear doing.

We finally found such a metaphor through conversations with midwives, nurses, and pediatricians. The "midwife metaphor" focuses attention on the *event* of leadership, rather than the *characteristics* of leadership.

Midwives are visionaries.	Midwives exercise a strong physical, spiritual, and psychological presence before, during, and after the birth process. The primary role of the midwife is to bring the mother to the event of delivery. The work of the midwife is to nurture the mother before, during, and after the birth, empowering her to overcome any discomfort or fear, so that she might surrender to the natural feelings of childbirth. The midwife moves "heaven and heart" to help a mother experience the awesome potential of birth.
Midwives are synthesizers.	Midwives are required during training to read all the books on birthing that obstetricians must read. However, their most important skill cannot be developed by study. They must be able to read and act on the clues revealed by the expectant mother herself. The clues from the mother give meaning to the textbook. The midwife synthesizes an enormous variety of data in a brief time and knows intuitively what to do.
Midwives are motivators.	Midwives never ask the expectant mother if she *wants* to give birth. They know that she

must give birth, or die. They do not say, *"If you want me to, I'll help you."* They know that the person wants them to help, even if it hurts. They encourage, coach, and empower. Their passion is not to do whatever the expectant mother wants to do. Their passion is not to birth a *boy* or a *girl,* nor is it to impose a career on the newly born child. Their passion is simply and single-mindedly to help others bring out the potential that God has created within them. Nothing gets in the way of this passion.

Spiritual Redwoods are led by Spiritual Midwives. They do whatever is necessary to facilitate the potential for birth that lies within others. Birth is the most profound and dynamic experience of "synergy" possible. Synergy means *the combined or cooperative action of two or more agents that together increases each other's effectiveness.* The results of synergy will always be more than merely the sum of the parts. In the experience of birth, mother and father, doctor and nurse, all combine and cooperate in a way that increases one another's effectiveness. The outcome—the newborn child—will be far more than the sum of all the personalities and talents involved in the birth. In fact, the synergy that allows birth to happen will include many other agents beyond the parents, doctors, and nurses. The administrators who maintain the hospital, the researchers who create new techniques and medicines, the custodial staff who cleanse the delivery room, and even the unknown taxi driver who rushed the expectant mother to the hospital all play their part. The complexity of the synergy of birth involves practical and emotional, physical and spiritual elements. The midwife is the leader who gathers all the elements together, and guides the combinations of energies, in order for life to be born. If birth is a profound synergy, then the midwife is a capable "synergist." The "synergist" enhances the synergy of life.

> Spiritual midwives can see in others what others have not seen in themselves.

All people, male or female, young or old, are "expectant mothers," whether they know it or not. God has created every person with gifts and callings, and every person carries the inner potential to be fulfilled as God's child. Midwives protect the mother from outside distractions and coach the mother to breathe. Spiritual midwives help "the expectant" to concentrate and coach "the expectant" in spiritual disciplines. Midwives resist every inclination of the mother to become dependent on them for the care of the newborn baby. Spiritual midwives resist every inclination of Christians to become dependent on them for the exercise of newborn ministry. Such leaders know that the role of the midwife is to cut the cord and hand the new life back to the one who birthed it. They are not afraid to get out of the way of new life, because they are convinced that the fullness of truth lies ever beyond themselves.

The church leaders of Christendom have become personal chaplains who move from room to room, or house to house, "taking care" of individuals in the church. They attend every committee meeting, answer every telephone call, and rush to the side of anyone who beckons to them. They play the game of "pastor-fetch," enabling individuals and congregations to do whatever they want to do. Spiritual midwives do not "take care" of people. They avoid codependencies that make the laity perpetually needy and the pastor perpetually needed. Spiritual midwives help individuals and congregations birth the potential God has placed within them, and then cut the cord to hand new life back to the one who birthed it. The spiritual midwife cannot know, and will not control, the future of the mystery that has been born.

Spiritual midwives read all the scriptural, theological, and historical material they can, but their most important skills cannot be learned in seminary. They purposely involve themselves in conversation with the cultural "forest," spending as much time with seekers beyond the congregation as they do with disciples within the congregation. Midwives sit long hours listening to the fears and dreams of the parents-to-be. Spiritual midwives spend long hours listening to the yearnings and dreams of the public. Midwives monitor the heartbeat for fetal heart tones and maternal pulses. Spiritual midwives observe people and monitor cultural trends. Midwives look for signs of dehydration and fatigue. Spiritual midwives look for hidden crises and emerging needs. These leaders continually look for new ways to build significant connections with others. They synthesize an enormous diversity of data and discover fresh insights and new opportunities.

The church leaders of Christendom have become institutional power brokers who are preoccupied by the internal affairs of the group. Only they understand the intricate denominational polities, subtle congregational politics, and historically nuanced worship of the faith community. They deliberately do *not* venture among the public, unless it is to represent the institution as its spokesperson. Sharing coffee with complete strangers in a bar, coffee shop, or sports arena is "time off" from their "true" work. Spiritual midwives routinely and purposely place themselves among the publics beyond congregational life. Not only can they perceive the emerging needs of the people, but through the eyes of outsiders they can "take the pulse" of congregational life with greater accuracy and honesty. They bring to the synergy of birth a larger synthesis of reality and yearning.

Spiritual midwives do not ask people where they want to go and then simply help them get there. They do not ask if people want them to lead. They know that people want them to lead. They listen to the hopes and dreams of people in their midst, sense the potential that lies within them, and then take action to help them overcome pain and fear in order to experience the joy of birth. Midwives encourage and motivate a mother to do more then she thinks she can do. Spiritual midwives encourage and motivate people to be more than they think they are. Midwives laugh and weep with expectant mothers in labor, empowering them with excitement and joy. Spiritual midwives laugh and weep amid the struggles of others, empowering them with excitement and joy. The only two choices are *to give birth*, or *to witness death*. Even when "the expectant" cries out in pain and asks to stop, the midwife coaxes, assures, and perpetually leads toward birth. They are not called to witness death. They are called to help birth life. In the midst of the worst pain, they say "push."

The church leaders of Christendom exert power over others. They rely on ordination, office, and superior knowledge in order to organize people to fulfill the institutional purpose that is their personal agenda. The heritage of the church and the purposes of the institution cannot be compromised, even if it means the ultimate death of the congregation itself. Such leaders would rather retire than let go of control, and they nurture churches that would rather close than change. Spiritual midwives lead by relational influence. They rely on their own authenticity and enthusiasm for life, which engages others for a common purpose of spiritual growth. They contribute to the well-being of others through mutual consent and respect. These leaders always have an agenda. But it is God's agenda for life. It is God's agenda for discipleship.

The "midwife metaphor" affirms the importance of an individual to give leadership in the church, but more than this it affirms the importance of the "leadership event" that is a mutual relationship of trust and respect. Both the midwife and the expectant mother have a role to play in the birth of new life. Both the Spiritual midwife and the "spiritually expectant" person have a role to play in the birth of new ministry. Neither the "dictator" (through power, authority, or coercion) nor the "enabler" (through correct information, group process, and goodwill) can help anyone birth new life. Spiritual midwives and "the Expectant" enter into relationships of trust, in which the leader may be alternately urgent and patient, challenging and nurturing. This mutual trust and respect that frees leaders to play many different roles in congregational life and mission is the "leadership event" that typifies the Spiritual Redwood.

> Neither the dictator nor the enabler helps anyone birth new life.

The "midwife metaphor" has many nuances that we have only begun to explore. The more we observe this new species of leader among the Spiritual Redwoods of the twenty-first-century pre-Christian era, the more we see connections with the church builders of the first-century pre-Christian era. Here are some specific clues that it provides for leadership in the twenty-first century.

1. Spiritual midwives are grown . . . not born or made. Such leadership emerges from an experience of life in which individuals have been helped by another to blossom into life. People are not *born* to be Spiritual midwives, nor are people *trained* to be Spiritual midwives. One cannot deny the calling by saying that *"God didn't create me*

that way!" Nor can one embrace the calling by asking, *"What cur-riculum or training course can I take to do it?"* One becomes a Spiritual midwife through being touched by a Spiritual midwife.

Even so, Paul grows to become a missionary who can give birth to other Christian leaders only through his own experience of the spiritual guidance and coaching of Ananias (Acts 9). His change along the Damascus road is not the key to his future mission. It is the mentoring of Ananias that ultimately allows the Gentile mission to be born, and which alone empowers Paul to climb over the physical walls of the city, and the metaphorical walls of heritage, and let loose his enthusiasm in the world.

The only reason we can help others give birth to their potential, is that someone in our past helped us give birth to our potential.

2. The primary role of the Spiritual midwife is to create an environment in which people are encouraged to give birth to the potential God has created within them. They see within others a hidden potential given by God that is greater than the potential others see in themselves. They perceive new life that is waiting to be born. They do not understand themselves to be "corporate directors" or "caregivers," but they are passionate to help others bring new life into the world.

Even so, the mission to the Gentiles takes no prescribed pattern and imposes no standardized institutional expectations. The male and female Christian leaders in Jerusalem impose few restrictions on the new believers of the Gentile world (Acts 15). Instead, they create environments of intimacy, prayer, reflection about Scripture, and spiritual discipline that can give birth to new communities of faith (Acts 16).

Spiritual midwives create systems in which people can grow in faith and release creative energies for ministry.

3. Spiritual midwives always celebrate freedom. Their ultimate joy is to watch "the newborn" begin life utterly dependent on another human being and then grow to be completely free to be whatever God created the person to be. Everything they do either builds upon, or leads to, transformation and growth. They do not want people to be dependent on them; nor do they want to do things for others that others can do themselves; nor do they want to dictate to others how to live their lives.

Even so, Paul and Silas equip Lydia and her friends to become the true ministers of the growing church of Philippi. The most profound miracle is not the earthquake that shakes the foundations of the city, nor is it the faith that is born in former jailors and prisoners. The most profound miracle is that Paul and Silas *get out of the way.* They leave. They move on. They help Lydia give birth to the potential God has given her, and then step aside so that she can do it in her own creative way.

Spiritual midwives equip others for leadership, relinquish control, and rejoice to see new life move in unexpected and creative new ways.

4. Spiritual midwives lead by authenticity and influence. They lead from their own experience of life struggle and spiritual victory, and influence the lives of others by their example and practical support. Unlike the "dictator," they do not try to coerce others by using authoritative offices. Unlike the "enabler," they do not try to manage others by using bureaucracy and group process. Entitlements and certifications are not important to leadership. Credibility, trustworthiness, spirituality, and practicality are the foundations for effective leadership.

Even so, Lydia leads the Philippian church out of her own authenticity of change and growth. Paul does not tell her what to do, but encourages her own self-confidence (Phil. 1:6). The growing midwives of Philippi are encouraged to ground their leadership in the worthiness of their own lives (1:27), and in their own experiences of transformation through relationship with Jesus (3:12).

They are ready to embrace change with the same enthusiasm with which one embraces a loved one. They are prepared to risk their own security for the sake of that joy.

ROSA PARKS

Rosa Parks is a role model for the twenty-first century. Her leadership was validated by her cultural credibility and courageous example, not by an office or a credential. Her life became a "leadership event."

In 1955, she boarded a bus in Montgomery, Alabama, paid her fare, and sat in the first row of the black section of the bus. When the front seats of the bus filled, the driver told the black passengers to move so that a white passenger could sit down. Rosa Parks refused to move.

Her subsequent arrest resulted in the 381-day bus boycott that catapulted another "spiritual midwife," Martin Luther King, Jr., into leadership. Eleven months later, her action prompted the Supreme Court to rule that segregation on public transportation was unconstitutional.

Of course, the struggle for civil rights is far from over, but she set the process of freedom in motion. As of 1996, Rosa Parks is eighty-three and still draws a crowd.

5. **Spiritual midwives are always servants.** They readily do work that is hard, dirty, or seemingly trivial. The tools of midwifery are towels, menstrual pads, plastic gloves and trash bags, and diapers. Giving birth is a wet and messy experience. Spiritual midwives may be regarded by denominational professionals as second-class competition. People ask them for assistance motivated by urgent crisis and recognition of practical competence.

Even so, Jesus equips the spiritual leadership of the disciples by wearing a towel and washing their feet (John 13). It is an example they will imitate in mission. The same people who share the gospel also wait on tables (Acts 7). The same "apostle to the Gentiles" also makes tents for a living and troubles himself with Onesimus the slave (Philemon).

Spiritual midwives seek no high status or special privilege. They are there to help others become the "royalty" of God.

6. Spiritual midwives "have a Bible in one hand and a pom-pom in the other." They are the most sympathetic of all comforters and the most encouraging of all cheerleaders. Midwives spend hours pouring water over the mother's pregnant abdomen to aid relaxation, rub the mother's feet, breathe as she breathes, keeping her from being overwhelmed with the changes that are taking place within her. Spiritual midwives do the same for "the Expectant" in their midst. When others are down, they lift them up. When others are lazy, they prod them forward.

Even so, the legacy of the Christian leaders to the early church was not their personal biographies, but the memory of their companionship. We know little about them. We know much about their companionship with others. Their letters are filled with encouragement and advice. They are the most sympathetic of comforters, and also the most challenging of all prophets.

Spiritual midwives spend most of their time encouraging, coaching, mentoring, and guiding people to their own personal destiny with God.

The leader of the Spiritual Redwood will spend the most time with those most likely to carry on the vision of transformation. In other words, the Spiritual midwife will spend the most time with those who can, through their own experience of birth, become Spiritual midwives to others. Look at the ministry of Jesus. Jesus concentrated his efforts on Peter, James, and John . . . then on the Twelve . . . then on the Seventy. They became the ones who then ministered in myriad ways to the multitudes.

Jesus either ignored the bureaucrats and the complainers, or he went out of his way to upset them. The last thing on his mind was to do their bidding or shape his ministry around their agenda. Spiritual midwives invest their time mentoring a few, who in turn invest their time transforming others.

The leader of the Spiritual Redwood will spend the most time with the people who are healthy enough to birth new life. In the age of Christendom, many pastors spent more than 80 percent of their time with dysfunctional people. After seven years of ministry, a pastor might easily spend most of his or her energy with only five families of the church! Even denominational leaders may spend 80 percent of their time with dysfunctional churches. All this directs energy toward the wrong priorities. It is as if the midwife were spending all her time with those who could not give birth! This does not mean anyone should be ignored, or that Spiritual Redwoods will not care for their most needy members. It simply means that the Spiritual midwife is not the one to do these ministries. This leader must empower those healthy enough to birth new life.

Spiritual midwives build teams. Hierarchy is nearly eliminated and mutual cooperation is enhanced. No single person is always the "director," and no single person is always the "gopher." Each member of the team is indispensable to the team, and the wholeness of each person is dependent on the wholeness of the others. Together they form a powerful influence in congregation and community. Their roles vary as the missions evolve. Now one staff person leads, and now another staff person leads, and now all the staff follow the leadership of a volunteer. Leaders of Spiritual Redwoods empower each team member to be as strong as they can be.

Spiritual Redwoods always have a strong leader who is a visionary, a synthesizer, and a motivator. The "midwife metaphor" helps us perceive "the person within the tree." These leaders live for the event called "birth"! Administration, management, chaplaincy, and pastoral care are all gifts that can be incorporated into many ministries, but the primary role of the leader of the Spiritual Redwood is none of these. The role of the leader is to help others experience the event of transformation.

Spiritual midwives are "synergists." They build the synergy that leads to life—and they celebrate the fact that life always builds new synergy. In the transition time between the post-Christendom era and the pre-Christian era, churches suffer in three ways:

"*Barrenness*": Churches refuse to change and grow. They believe their heritage has made them "complete," and that they are not called to venture into new mysteries and possibilities. They are barren, not by nature, but by choice. They refuse to give birth to something new.

"*Abortion*": Churches birth something new—and then kill it. New energy, new mission, new ministry, new ideas, or new leadership emerges in the church. Yet the church fears that creativity and allows it

| | to die. Under-resourced and under-supported, ministries and leaders slip away from the church that cannot take risks. |
| *"Stillbirth":* | Churches experience incredible agony, or expend enormous bureaucratic energy, only to give birth to a program that is already dead. It is irrelevant to the real needs of people, and it fails to articulate the gospel in ways that are accessible by the public. All the argument and planning ultimately creates only one more variation of the past, rather than birthing something truly original. |

Spiritual midwives will not accept these options. They believe that God does not accept these options. They are wholly committed to birth. Life only thrives when it is given away! Life only thrives when people take risks and celebrate mysteries! Life only thrives when churches embrace change and are willing to let go of control and allow that which is newly born to find its own way!

Three Keys to Twenty-First-Century Leadership

The revolution of spiritual leadership in the pre-Christian, twenty-first century returns the church to the leadership paradigms of the Acts of the Apostles. This revolution involves three key leadership changes that may be deeply stressful for twentieth-century church leadership based on the paradigms of institutional entitlements common to the church since the age of Constantine. The leadership that is crucial to the Spiritual Redwoods growing in the twenty-first century dramatically models these key changes.

1. Spiritual midwives communicate to others *the immediacy of God.* Pre-Christian people must see in their spiritual leaders the living proof of the difference Jesus can make in their lives. Authenticity is grounded in daily living, not in the professional presentation of sermons, the artistry of the worship service, or the construction of mission statements. Unlike post-Constantinian church leadership, the new spiritual leadership cannot represent the Holy as "Priest," nor can it authoritatively speak for the Holy as

"Preacher." Like the leadership of the Acts of the Apostles, spiritual midwives must empower others to experience for themselves the immediacy of God.

Church leadership in the post-Constantinian age was all about creating mediated experiences of God and nurturing controllable experiences of the Holy. Church leaders created and repeated liturgies, authoritatively interpreted Scripture, enforced traditional practices, maintained institutional structures, and instructed spiritual "amateurs" about right and wrong.

Spiritual leadership in the pre-Christian, twenty-first century is very different. It communicates the *immediacy* of God that overflows the institutional conduits that sought to control access to the ocean of God's grace, or which tried to impose standardized interpretations on the experience of that grace. The spiritual midwife recognizes that the waters of grace are like the waters that surround the fetus in the womb. These waters act as a lubricant, as a propellant, that carries the fetus from the womb in an uncontrollable rush of birth. It is the "hydrostatic wedge" that eases the body of the newborn forward in the birth canal. Spiritual midwives recognize that the holy is not controllable; it can only be "cope-able." They do not control birth. They can only help "the Expectant" ones cope with the ecstasy.

Spiritual midwives carry within themselves the immediate experience of God. They have been transformed by God through connection with Jesus. They have not only heard about burning bushes that are never consumed, they have *seen* burning bushes that are never consumed! They not only repeat stories of the prophets who have seen cherubim and received hot coals pressed to their lips, but they have *experienced* hot coals pressed to their lips! Their authenticity is not communicated by practiced and prepared sermons that demonstrate their knowledge of religious experience. Their authenticity is communicated through unrehearsed, spontaneous words and deeds that reveal their hearts.

Spiritual midwives help others break out to the immediate experience of God. They help people sever their dependence on mediated religion, to discover their own experience of God in entirely fresh and individual ways. They help people sever any dependencies they may have formed on the clergy, the church leaders, or even the spiritual midwives! Not even the spiritual leader can be allowed to control or mediate the Holy. Such leaders empower others to plunge into spiritual depths, or prepare others to be unpredictably overwhelmed by mystery.

Spiritual midwives help people assess their uncontrollable experiences of the Holy. Not only is the immediate experience of God often unexpected; it may well be positively bizarre! The unusual, the different, the odd, the abnormal, the irrational, and the bizarre all emerge powerfully in the pre-Christian era. The experiences of early New Testament Christians were often bizarre. They only seem "normal" now because Christians have read the stories so often. The point is that not all that is bizarre is therefore authentically of God, and not all that is mundane is therefore devoid of revelatory truth! Christian faith does not have to be crazy to be true—but neither does it have to be boring to be authentic!

In the post-Constantinian era, methodologies of Scripture, Reason, Experience, and Tradition helped interpret the mediated experiences of God. In the pre-Christian era, spiritual leaders must do more in order to communicate, empower, and discern immediate experiences of God. They draw upon all six of the great spiritual movements of Christianity:

- Scriptural wisdom and life transformation from the "evangelical movement"
- Moral integrity and ethical witness from the "social justice movement"
- Personal purity and inner virtue from the "holiness movement"
- Gifts and ecstatic joy from the "charismatic movement"
- Corporate celebration and mutual support from the "liturgical renewal movement"
- Listening and intuition from the "contemplative movement."

The unity of all six "movements" in the spiritual leadership of the twenty-first century makes those leaders appear quite eclectic, versatile, or flexible to the public. And they are often treated with some suspicion from within denominations which defined themselves as representing one movement over against others. Spiritual midwives are the "synthesizers" of the pre-Christian age and the "misfits" of past Christendom.

2. Spiritual leadership integrates *Spiritual Life and Spiritual Calling.* Unlike post-Constantinian church leadership, there can be no distinction between "office" and "person," or between "professional" and "private" life. Like the leaders in the Acts of the Apostles, spiritual leaders purposely exercise their calling to model and interpret the spiritual life from their own daily living.

Spiritual midwives integrate spiritual life and spiritual calling in a way that blurs all former distinctions between "person" and "profession." Such leadership does not calculate work hours against time off. Spiritual sensitivity to the immediacy of God pervades each moment of each day. It is reflected in the planned actions and words of leadership, but it is even more powerfully revealed through the unplanned actions and words of daily living. The unplanned action and the spontaneous comment reveal the real truth about one's leadership, and are the true test in the eyes of the pre-Christian public for any leader's authenticity. Spiritual leadership is less a matter of *doing* than it is a matter of *being*.

> There is no distinction between office and person, professional and private life, clergy and laity, leader and follower.

Spiritual Life and Spiritual Calling are twin, mutually reinforcing, movements of Spiritual Leadership. Each is a life process, not merely a state of being or pattern of activity. Spiritual Life begins with *radical humility*. Such humility is "radical" because it is more than an attitude of modesty, and quite different from mere self-deprecation. Edwin Freedman implies such humility when describing the "self-differentiated person." *Radical humility* means a profound versatility in social participation and self-understanding. It is the ability to play many different roles, without ever losing one's own sense of identity. Just as early Christian monastics could be priest, politician, reformer, mystic, pilgrim, martyr, and friend, so also the radical humility of spiritual leaders allows them to be passive or aggressive, modest or bombastic, shy or charismatic.

Radical humility is only possible in the context of the immediacy of God. One can be remarkably versatile, without losing identity, only through a heightened awareness of the Holy which lies beyond the self. The objectivity of the Holy that lies beyond the self, but with which the self is intimately connected, both motivates and limits multiple roles of social participation. Spiritual leaders simultaneously have the audacity to criticize and the courage to admit mistakes. They are continuously learning and growing, sometimes at great cost to themselves.

The next step in the Spiritual Life is *thoughtful reflection*. It is the ability to understand and assess the hidden influences that shape one's own thought and action. It is the ability simultaneously to analyze and synthesize, eliminating groundless prejudices and needless contradictions, and creating an ever larger coherence in life. *Thoughtful reflection* does not aim to explain away mystery, but to allow mystery to "make sense" in daily living.

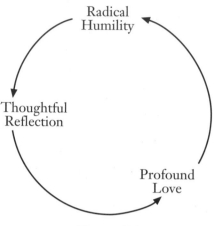

SPIRITUAL LIFE

Radical Humility

Thoughtful Reflection

Profound Love

Figure 7.3

Thoughtful reflection provides spiritual leadership with its risk-taking or entrepreneurial character. The continuous possibility of "being wrong" that is revealed in radical humility, is countered with a profound trust in the immediate experience of God. That trust is not a certainty about being right, but a confidence about being ultimately accepted by God even when wrong.

The next step in the Spiritual Life is *profound love*. Such love is "profound" because it arises only from the discipline of the first two steps. Only then can love endure the stress of real life and grow beyond mere sentimentality. Profound love has less to do with good feelings between people, than with moral responsibilities shared by people. It is simultaneously self-sacrificial and self-affirming, because the richness of life that has been gained by an individual only endures if it is given away to others.

Profound love provides spiritual midwives with their extraordinary courage and boundless joy. It rescues the spiritual life from passivity. It motivates the will and pushes one to act with urgency. It pushes trust to the farthest limits of generosity. Love becomes profound when it gives equal priority to strangers beyond the sphere of church life. Love becomes profound when leadership releases control over others, and instead equips others to discover new life for themselves.

Love necessarily involves pain and mystery, just as love led Jesus to the cross. Suffering is then filled with new meaning, and the spiritual midwife is once again filled with awe for the greatness of God. Therefore, the spiritual leader returns to *radical humility* once again, and the cycle of the spiritual life is repeated over and over again. Spiritual midwives embrace the maxim of Jesus: "Those who want to save their life will lose it, and those who lose their life for my sake, and for the sake of the gospel, will save it" (Mark 8:35).

Spiritual Calling is the twin, mutually reinforcing, movement of leadership that parallels and connects with Spiritual Life. Spiritual Calling begins with *the intuition of the Holy.* Such intuition may be occasionally dramatic, but it is constantly pervasive. Elijah may occasionally have heard "still, small voices," but more often he was scanning the distant horizon and inner heart for clues to the guidance of God. Spiritual midwives are committed to more than prayer and seem perpetually to be listening for God. Spiritual midwives deliberately place themselves in a wide variety of contexts, yet with heightened sensitivities. They have the ability to appreciate many different perspectives, without losing their sense of destiny.

The next step in Spiritual Calling is *cultural perceptiveness.* This is the ability to discern the contradictions and opportunities that are emerging through cultural change, and the gaps of continuity between people, power, and meaning. Spiritual midwives are constantly looking beyond the business of the church, studying the direction and flow of daily life. They understand that culture itself, in all its complexities and

SPIRITUAL CALLING

Figure 7.4

nuances, can become a vehicle for eternal truth. Therefore, they have the ability to experiment boldly, without losing sight of their ultimate goals.

The next step in Spiritual Calling is *compassion for the lost*. The profound love of the spiritual life is intensified and focused toward those who do not have any connection with God (whether immediate or mediated). Spiritual midwives integrate all six of the great spiritual movements of Christianity in order to bring to bear the particular grace most needed by the lost:

- guidance and conviction for the seekers
- vindication and social reform for the oppressed
- cleansing and healing for the broken
- self-discovery and hope for the stressed
- mutual support and friendship for the alienated
- serenity, courage, and wisdom for the addicted.

Spiritual midwives have the ability to become intimate companions with those who do not have a connection with God, without losing their own connection with Jesus.

Companionship with the lost inevitably stretches the imagination and challenges both strategies and assumptions. This returns the spiritual midwife to the original intuition of the Holy that is the core vision for what she or he does. With renewed conviction, the cycle of spiritual calling is repeated over and over again. Spiritual midwives embrace the words of Jesus: "You did not choose me but I chose you. And I appointed you to go and bear fruit" (John 15:16).

3. Spiritual leadership unites "ally" and "leader" in *a wholeness of mutual support*. Unlike post-Constantinian church leadership, there can be no separation between "laity" and "clergy," or between "church" and "church leader," or between "follower" and "instructor." Like the leaders in the Acts of the Apostles, spiritual midwives emerge from, and recede into, the Body of Christ as the Spirit beckons.

Together, these twin, mutually reenforcing processes are the essence of the spiritual midwife. As seen in figure 7.5 each process is described by a helix. The person moves through the process and returns to the beginning of the process once again. Together, the two processes intertwine as a "double helix" that resembles a strand of DNA:

Spiritual Event
Genetic Code

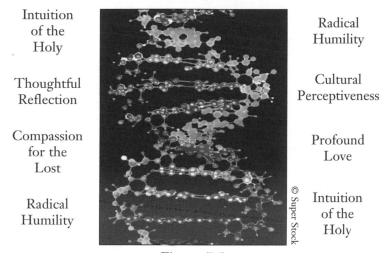

Intuition of the Holy	Radical Humility
Thoughtful Reflection	Cultural Perceptiveness
Compassion for the Lost	Profound Love
Radical Humility	Intuition of the Holy

© Super Stock

Figure 7.5

In the Spiritual Redwoods growing in the pre-Christian, twenty-first century, this double-helix of spiritual life and spiritual calling *is the DNA that defines the "genetic identity" of this new species of the Body of Christ.* Each part of the Body of Christ, no matter how small or seemingly insignificant, carries within itself this same "genetic code." The "genetic code" of the church is the double helix of Spiritual Life and Spiritual Calling. Not only does the pastor carry within himself or herself this "genetic code" of spiritual leadership, but so also do the church secretary and the custodian . . . and so also do the administrators and small group leaders . . . and so also do the individual members and adherents. Everyone, old or young, veteran or newcomer, carries this same "genetic signature" that identifies that person as belonging to the Spiritual Redwood.

This means that the very terminology of "spiritual *leadership*" becomes inadequate to describe the dynamic life of the Spiritual Redwood! Spiritual leadership has been transformed into the wholeness of mutual support and spontaneous outreach originally revealed in the earliest church. That is why we prefer the metaphor "Spiritual Midwife." Leadership is not a list of characteristics. It is an experience. It is an event.

You see, in the post-Constantinian church, distinctions quickly emerged between "clergy" and "laity," or between "congregation" and "church leader." The very term "leader" assumes a counterpart "follower," and these two roles have gained institutional legitimacy and permanence over the centuries of Christendom. "Leaders" might pursue a spiritual life, but "followers" do not. "Clergy" might have spiritual callings, but "laity" do not. "Ministers" might do "ministry," but "laity" only do "management." For this reason, many people have gone into "the Ministry" simply because they wanted to be in *a* ministry and felt this was the only way to do it. Yet the Scriptures know nothing about "the Ministry" and make no distinctions between clergy and laity.

One might say that the "genetic code" that distinguished the identity of the institutional leader came to be understood as being quite different from the "genetic code" that identified the followers. This inner difference was visibly marked and celebrated. Clergy wore vestments, and laity did not. Clergy held entitled offices, and laity did not. Clergy were ordained and commissioned, and laity were not. Clergy initiated liturgies, and laity responded to liturgies. Clergy preached, and laity listened. Clergy led civil rights marches, and laity raised the money to allow them to do it. In a hundred subtle ways the era of Christendom entrenched the belief that "leaders" and "followers" were *inherently different.*

All Christians carry the same genetic code.

Spiritual Redwoods grow in a different kind of forest, one that has not been seen for nearly 2,000 years. Christendom is dead, and with it the institutionalized distinctions of leadership. The pre-Christian era has begun, and with it a whole new understanding of leadership.

Spiritual Redwoods in the twenty-first century remove the distinctions of leadership, to build one dynamic wholeness of mutual support and spontaneous outreach. Every member of the organism carries the double helix of Spiritual Life and Spiritual Calling. It is the genetic signature that has replaced institutional membership as the sign of belonging. Every part of the Body of Christ becomes a Spiritual Midwife, bubbling up in timely ways, as the Spirit beckons. They emerge from the Body of Christ, and recede into the Body of Christ, only to emerge once more in other directions and in other ways. The Body of Christ for the twenty-first century is not an institution, but a living organism. Each cell has a regenerative capacity to replace itself in ministry and then be reabsorbed into the body.

> In that renewal there is no longer Greek and Jew, circumcised and uncircumcised, barbarian, Scythian, slave and free; but Christ is all and in all! (Col. 3:11)

In the same way there is no longer clergy and laity, expert and amateur, leader and follower, preacher and listener, teacher and student, caregiver and care-receiver, entitled offices and ordinary folks . . . *"but Christ is all and in all!"*

Only one thing characterizes the heart and soul of the Spiritual Redwood. They exist to set people free from whatever bondage holds them. They exist to assist people on the journey with God. Transformation is at the heart of these spiritual organisms. This means that the experience of birth and the presence of the spiritual midwife are inseparable. When you gaze upon the Spiritual Redwood and a human face emerges from the tree, you have not met the Executive Director . . . *you have encountered the core transformational event.*

VISTA EIGHT

The Tree of Life

The Essence of the Future

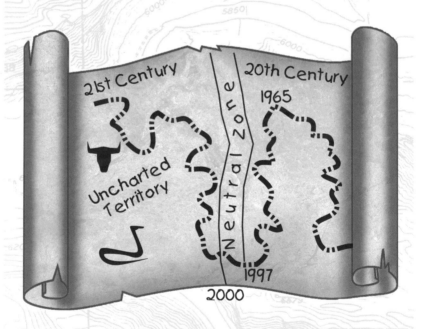

At last,
the horizon can begin to be seen.

T *he Redwood grows in a different kind of forest. This forest is constantly changing, growing, and advancing. The noises within it are many and beautiful, but often strange . . . mysteries in conversation with mysteries. Colors and smells struggle to capture the senses . . . and influence behavior. Mutations multiply, and every moment gives birth to a whole new species of organism.*

This forest is not like the parklands of the now decaying city. There are no carefully marked bicycle paths, nor are there any paved and lighted walkways. This forest is not like the woodlots of the settled, slowly depopulating countryside. The underbrush grows thick and invades plowed fields on every side. This forest is not like the controlled environments of national wilderness parks. There are no designated campsites, and wild animals may leap out at any time. This new forest is extraordinarily alive, and well-managed civilization recedes before it.

The Redwoods tower above it. . . . always in clusters, with intertwined roots for stability. As one blazes a trail through the forest, the Redwood can be a visual guide. As one comes still closer, the scent of the organism beckons one forward. As one emerges into the clearing, noticing the size, the shade, the complexity of branches, and the abundance of fruits, one marvels that the redwood has integrated all the diversity of the forest into a single great purpose.

This is more than a tree. This is an entire ecosystem of harmony, safety, and growth, in which every creature and every organism can thrive in its own unique way. One cannot help being assured and welcomed.

This is more than a tree. This is an event in which every creature and organism has been granted asylum in the midst of the forest, and is fed, nurtured, and transformed. One cannot help being challenged and empowered.

This is a Tree of Life. It draws upon life, nurtures life, and births new life. The cycle from seed, to growth, to flower, and to seed again is neverending.

But now . . . climb the tree! Climb higher and higher, to a dizzying height, and look around you. Now you can see a bigger picture, a bigger vision, than ever before. You can see where the forest fires are raging, and where the watersheds are located. You can see mountains and valleys. You can see where sections of the forest are uniquely different from other sections of the forest. You can see where the forest is going.

Never have you felt more exhilarated, and yet, swaying as you are in the wind, never have you felt less secure. You are in the midst of a great purpose, a giant synthesis, a powerful witness. What does it matter if every moment is a risk? What does it matter if you fall? There are many branches beneath ready to catch you. The Redwood itself is an assurance that change . . . constant change . . . is good. God's purpose is not survival, but growth. You are not just seeing a view. You are living a vision!

If churches were "machines"—and church participants were merely assorted officeholders, committee members, converts, offering envelope holders, and other statistical "cogs and wheels" for the "machine"—then optimum quality of life could be described as "energy efficiency." The quest for quality would focus leadership on lubricating wheels, eliminating redundancy, repairing short circuits, and increasing service for broken, worn out, or defective parts of the machine. Leadership in the organizational machines of Christendom did just that. They lubricated the nominations and management processes of the church, distributed permission-giving power among key middle managers, committed enormous energy to troubleshooting communication breakdowns and conflicts, and spent most of their time with people who were broken, worn out, or otherwise unable to contribute to the smooth operations of the organization.

However, if churches are "organisms"—and participants are spiritually growing persons with diverse tastes and lifestyles, personal needs and spiritual yearnings—then optimum quality of life can best be described as "good health." The quest for quality will focus leadership on planting seeds, fertilizing soil, nurturing growth, and enhancing the opportunities for every root, twig, and leaf to stretch out into the environment. Leaders in the organisms of Spiritual Redwoods do just this. They envision new life, encourage individual initiative, nurture personal discovery and spiritual growth, and enhance the abilities of all persons to give birth to the potential God has created within them. The power of the *midwife* metaphor for twenty-first-century Christian leadership lies in the fact that the Body of Christ is an *organism*, and that optimum quality of life is a matter of *healthy spiritual growth*.

The *Tree of Life* is an ancient symbol. It is so called because its fruit conferred health, long life, success, and happiness to those who ate it. In ancient Mesopotamia, Gilgamesh acquired a plant from the bottom of the sea. It was pictured as a date palm—the most important, life-giving tree of a desert economy. In ancient

Assyria, the tree was pictured with wild goats, attracted to its safety and sustenance. In ancient Canaan, the tree was pictured as a grove of greenery associated with fertility and creation.

The *Tree of Life* was taken into the faith of Israel. The book of Genesis places the tree in the Garden of Eden, and the fruit from it gave immortality to Adam and Eve (Gen. 2:9). Proverbs associates the *Tree of Life* with true wisdom, or, in rabbinic tradition, the Torah:

> Her ways are ways of pleasantness,
>   and all her paths are peace.
> She is a tree of life to those who lay hold of her;
>   those who hold her fast are called happy. (Prov. 3:17-18)

The *Tree of Life* is said to offer the fruit of righteousness (Prov. 11:30), the fulfillment of hope and desire (Prov. 13:12), and a "gentle tongue" for counsel and personal support (Prov. 15:4). Adam and Eve are exiled from Eden after eating of the Tree of Knowledge, and the *Tree of Life* itself remains guarded. Yet the return to Eden to live in the presence of the *Tree of Life* remains a fundamental yearning of humankind. In the apocalyptic visions of Enoch and Esdras, the *Tree of Life* is promised to the righteous. It is a promise echoed in Revelation (22:14): "Blessed are those who wash their robes, so that they will have the right to the tree of life and may enter the city by the gates." The first Christians believed that through Jesus, the New Adam, we might "return to Eden," and "that the creation itself [would] be set free from its bondage to decay" (Rom. 8:21).

In the pre-Christian forest of the twenty-first century, we have recovered the insight of the Apostolic Age. We have eaten from the Tree of Knowledge . . . and we have manufactured the ecclesiastical machines of Christendom! Today we, too, yearn to return to Eden. We, too, yearn to enjoy the ecosystem of that *other* tree in Eden . . . the *Tree of Life!* God promises that in its environment lies the fulfillment of our yearnings. The river of the waters of life flows from the throne of God, and on either side of the river grows the *Tree of Life* . . . "and the leaves of the tree are for the healing of the nations" (Rev. 22:1, 2).

If the church is a foretaste of the realm of God, then Spiritual Redwoods are a premonition of the *Tree of Life*. Spiritual Redwoods have a passion for transformation, liberation, and life. It is their place in the ecosystem of the cultural forest. They have three primary processes in simultaneous action.

1. The inviting process . . .

- in which the continuing experiences of Jesus' interaction with the spiritual yearnings of people, in all its cultural diversity, are absorbed into the organism, and,
- in which spiritually yearning people are drawn into an environment of personal spiritual growth.

Spiritual Redwoods organize and train themselves for the purpose of inviting people into the story of God's love. They invite people to find new life, by giving life away to others.

2. The growth process . . .

- in which people discover themselves, and learn how to build deep, healthy relationships with others and with God, and,
- in which people discern their opportunities to give birth to the potential that God has given every human being.

Spiritual Redwoods organize and train themselves to help people grow. They focus on deepening relationships with God, as the necessary step to helping people live as God wants them to live.

3. The sending process . . .

- in which people actually give birth to the precious gifts within themselves, transforming their families, their relationships, their neighborhoods, and their society, and,
- in which people are motivated and equipped to take responsibility for the newborn creature of God they have become, nurturing new life in healthy ways.

Spiritual Redwoods organize and train themselves to release people into the unknown. They release control, free people from institutional servitude, and send them into creative ministries that will pass life on to others.

The Spiritual Redwood does not take from the cultural forest anything that it does not give back again a hundredfold. They never recruit people to do "church work." Instead, they invite people to take part in a journey with God from bondage to freedom. They grow people to pursue a journey with God into the unknown with confidence and hope. They empower people to surrender the security of the "sanctuary," the "institution," and the "clergy," to find their own incarnation of Jesus in the lives of people who have not yet experienced the gospel.

> Spiritual Redwoods give back to the forest more than they take.

Spiritual Redwoods are a different species of church. They are not denominations, or institutions, or machines. They are leaving behind the dilemmas of the twentieth century, which are the legacies of Christendom, and creating a fresh synthesis to meet the needs of a new age.

Deadlocked Christendom			*Creative Spiritual Redwoods*
Either "liberal"	*or*	"conservative"	Faith-sharing activists
Either the human Jesus	*or*	the divine Christ	The mysterious paradox of incarnation
Either traditional	*or*	nontraditional worship	Indigenous, multitracked worship
Either bureaucracy	*or*	anarchy	Creative chaos
Either committees	*or*	task groups	Cell groups and ministry teams
Either clergy	*or*	laity	Multiple, equipped lay ministries
Either leaders	*or*	followers	Leadership events
Either dictators	*or*	enablers	Spiritual midwives

Spiritual Redwoods may be in continuous conversation with the cultural forest, but they are influencing, changing, and guiding that forest in a multitude of ways.

The view from atop a Spiritual Redwood can be life-changing. From the top of this tree you can, indeed, see the future of forestry! The vistas of opportunity in ministry are breathtaking. Many church leaders who once visit and experience a Spiritual Redwood can never again be content with the denominational "machines" of Christendom. They have been captured by a new . . . and an ancient . . . vision of the *Tree of Life*.

This vision is the source from which all future creativity will flow. This vision lies at the heart of everything we will attempt with our lives. It is not here today, and then replaced by another "vision" in the next annual budget. It is a lifelong goal to which one passionately devotes all the energies of leadership. We have spoken of visions as a "Song in the Heart." The *Tree of Life* is the "Song in the Heart of Creation." Gazing about upon the vistas of ministry that can be the future of the church, one senses like Paul that "the whole creation has been groaning in labor pains until now" (Rom. 8:22), eager to give birth to the full potential God has given each creature of the cultural forest. It is a deeper, grander, gentler song:

> Hear, O Israel: The LORD is our God, the LORD alone. You shall love the LORD your God with all your heart, and with all your soul, and with all your might. (Deut. 6:4-5)

This is a vision worth dying for. It causes one to be impatient with inaction, delay, and procrastination. This vision is the answer to the only really important question in life: *"What is it about our experience with Jesus that this cultural forest cannot live without?"*

From the top of this tree, the landscape below looks far less forbidding. This vision of the *Tree of Life* overcomes all reservations. It communicates a kind of reckless courage. It reveals a perspective on life and eternity that is entirely unimagined, and then sears it into the human heart so that it will forever be "odd," "out of step," and "peculiar" among the remnants of Christendom. With the passage of time, the *Tree of Life* will make all things new.

Even when you climb down from the top of the tree, to set out again into the cultural forest, you move forward with a new resolve. Have you ever felt as if you were standing at the edge of a wide, deep canyon that seemed too wide to leap across . . . but a still, small voice within you said, *"Go for it!"*? You feel a primal urge to jump. Yet you hesitate, because it's a long way across and a long way down.

You try to ignore the urgings, but something inside you will neither allow you to turn back, nor to remain where you are. After all, you are tired of going around in circles. You are weary of bureaucratic deadends. And you know that God wants you to lead! You know that God has more in store for you than just recycling the saints, or taking care of members who don't want to grow. There

Figure 8.1: View from the Top of the Tree

must be something bigger, broader, wider, higher, and deeper in faith and ministry than what you are currently experiencing.

You know it's time to take the leap! Yet most of the forces which influence your personal and professional security shout "Don't jump! Be content with ministry as usual! Maintain the glorious heritage!" The closer we come to the twenty-first century, both the "urge" and the "dirge" will grow more powerful in the hearts of caring church leaders. It is only a matter of time before more of us take the leap of faith into a new and effective form of ministry.

If you are standing at the edge—feeling eager and hesitant, joyful and anxious—give thanks to God. You are standing at the edge of your future.

INDEX